Pentaho Data Integration Quick Start Guide

Create ETL processes using Pentaho

María Carina Roldán

BIRMINGHAM - MUMBAI

Pentaho Data Integration Quick Start Guide

Commissioning Editor: Amey Varangaonkar
Acquisition Editor: Siddharth Mandal
Content Development Editor: Kirk Dsouza
Technical Editor: Jinesh Topiwala
Copy Editor: Safis Editing
Project Coordinator: Hardik Bhinde
Proofreader: Safis Editing
Indexer: Rekha Nair
Graphics: Jason Monteiro
Production Coordinator: Shantanu Zagade

First published: August 2018

Production reference: 1280818

Published by Packt Publishing Ltd.
Livery Place
35 Livery Street
Birmingham
B3 2PB, UK.

ISBN 978-1-78934-332-8

www.packtpub.com

To my lovely kids.

– María Carina Roldán

`mapt.io`

Mapt is an online digital library that gives you full access to over 5,000 books and videos, as well as industry leading tools to help you plan your personal development and advance your career. For more information, please visit our website.

Why subscribe?

- Spend less time learning and more time coding with practical eBooks and Videos from over 4,000 industry professionals

- Improve your learning with Skill Plans built especially for you

- Get a free eBook or video every month

- Mapt is fully searchable

- Copy and paste, print, and bookmark content

PacktPub.com

Did you know that Packt offers eBook versions of every book published, with PDF and ePub files available? You can upgrade to the eBook version at `www.PacktPub.com` and as a print book customer, you are entitled to a discount on the eBook copy. Get in touch with us at `service@packtpub.com` for more details.

At `www.PacktPub.com`, you can also read a collection of free technical articles, sign up for a range of free newsletters, and receive exclusive discounts and offers on Packt books and eBooks.

Foreword

María Carina started writing her first books for Kettle (aka Pentaho Data Integration or PDI) beginners almost 10 years ago. Since then, the Kettle project and its community have been growing quickly and certainly; since those early days, the number of possibilities with the tool have been exploding. In certain ways, the graphical user interfaces have become much better, but the sheer power of doing all sorts of complex data integration tasks can been daunting to people who are just getting started. Books like the one you're reading now are excellent in giving you a leg up.

We also need books like this one because the world of information technology is changing ever faster in directions we scarcely could have predicted a decade ago. Cloud, big data, Streaming, NoSQL, the technological evolutions seem to come faster and faster, and the data contained in it needs to get integrated somehow. This book will get you closer to solving gnarly problems a lot faster.

Kettle is a tool with very few limitations living on the bleeding edge of a lot of technologies, and people have been telling me over the years how liberating that is as compared to other software that constantly needs to tell you how to accomplish certain tasks. This freedom is meant to allow us to do complex data integration work and never get stuck and always find a way to get the job done, no matter how hard that is. With this book, getting started in this complexity is not daunting anymore; it's fun. I'm so very happy that María Carina decided to write this book, and I'm wishing you a lot of fun on the path to success that she's putting you on.

Matt Casters
Kettle project founder
Chief Solutions Architect at Neo4j

Contributors

About the author

María Carina Roldán was born in Argentina and has a bachelor's degree in computer science.

She started working with Pentaho back in 2006. She spent all these years developing BI solutions, mainly as an ETL specialist, and working for different companies around the world.

Currently, she lives in Buenos Aires and works as an independent consultant. Carina is the author of *Learning Pentaho Data Integration 8 CE*, published by Packt in December 2017. She has also authored other books on *Pentaho*, all of them published by Packt.

> *I'd like to thank all my friends who support my work, the technical reviewers for their time and dedication, and the readers who have trusted me through the years.*

About the reviewer

Sahil Goyal is a developer residing in Hyderabad, India. He is an online trainer and consultant, teaching ETL development and SQL development to working professionals and students. Sahil has a keen interest in Pentaho Data Integration ETL development and has been working on it for several years in multiple contexts (consulting, freelancing, and contracting) and countries (India, the USA, Malaysia, and Spain), which has added professional value and experience to his career.

He is currently working for a multinational corporation based in Belgium as a data integration developer.

Thanks to my friends and family for their support and patience during those long working days. Especially to my mother, who always has a smile for me and has been by my side throughout my career to date.

Packt is searching for authors like you

If you're interested in becoming an author for Packt, please visit authors.packtpub.com and apply today. We have worked with thousands of developers and tech professionals, just like you, to help them share their insight with the global tech community. You can make a general application, apply for a specific hot topic that we are recruiting an author for, or submit your own idea.

Table of Contents

Preface

Pentaho Data Integration Quick Start Guide provides the guidance needed to get started with **Pentaho Data Integration** (**PDI**), covering the main features of the tool. The book shows the interactive features of the graphical designer, and explains the main ETL capabilities that the tool offers.

The book's content is based on PDI 8.1 **Community Edition** (**CE**), the latest version. However, it can be used with the **Enterprise Edition** (**EE**) as well. Many of the examples will also work with earlier versions of PDI.

Who this book is for

This book is a helpful guide for software developers, business intelligence analysts, IT students, and everyone involved or interested in developing ETL solutions, or more generally in performing any kind of data manipulation.

What this book covers

Chapter 1, *Getting Started with PDI*, presents the tool. This chapter includes instructions for installing PDI and gives you the opportunity to explore and configure the graphical designer (Spoon).

Chapter 2, *Getting Familiar with Spoon*, explains the fundamentals of working with Spoon by designing, debugging, and testing a transformation.

Chapter 3, *Extracting Data*, discusses getting and combining data from different sources. In particular, this chapter explains how to get data from files and databases.

Chapter 4, *Transforming Data*, explains how to transform data in many ways. Also, it explains how to get system information and predefined variables to be used as part of the data flow.

Chapter 5, *Loading Data*, explains how to save the output of transformations into files and databases. In addition, it explains how to load data into a datamart.

Chapter 6, *Orchestrating your Work*, shows how to organize your work through simple PDI jobs. You will learn how to use jobs to sequence tasks, deal with files, send emails, run DDL, and to carry out other useful tasks.

To get the most out of this book

PDI is a multiplatform tool, meaning that it can be installed and used under any operating system. The only prerequisite is to have JVM 1.8 installed. You will also need a good text editor, for example, Sublime III or Notepad ++. It's also recommended that you have access to a relational database. The examples in the book were built with PostgreSQL syntax, but you can adapt them to any other engine, as soon as there is a JDBC driver for it. Throughout the chapters, several internet links are provided to complement what is explained. Therefore, having an internet connection while reading is highly recommended.

Download the example code files

You can download the example code files for this book from your account at `www.packtpub.com`. If you purchased this book elsewhere, you can visit `www.packtpub.com/support` and register to have the files emailed directly to you.

You can download the code files by following these steps:

1. Log in or register at `www.packtpub.com`.
2. Select the **SUPPORT** tab.
3. Click on **Code Downloads & Errata**.
4. Enter the name of the book in the **Search** box and follow the onscreen instructions.

Once the file is downloaded, please make sure that you unzip or extract the folder using the latest version of:

- WinRAR/7-Zip for Windows
- Zipeg/iZip/UnRarX for Mac
- 7-Zip/PeaZip for Linux

The code bundle for the book is also hosted on GitHub at `https://github.com/PacktPublishing/Pentaho-Data-Integration-Quick-Start-Guide`. In case there's an update to the code, it will be updated on the existing GitHub repository.

We also have other code bundles from our rich catalog of books and videos available at `https://github.com/PacktPublishing/`. Check them out!

Download the color images

We also provide a PDF file that has color images of the screenshots/diagrams used in this book. You can download it here: `http://www.packtpub.com/sites/default/files/downloads/PentahoDataIntegrationQuickStartGuide_ColorImages.pdf`.

Conventions used

There are a number of text conventions used throughout this book.

`CodeInText`: Indicates code words in text, database table names, folder names, filenames, file extensions, pathnames, dummy URLs, user input, and Twitter handles. Here is an example: "You should specify the full path, for instance: `C:/Pentaho/data/ny_cities`."

A block of code is set as follows:

```
SELECT full_name
, injury_type
, to_char(start_date_time, 'yyyy-mm-dd') as injury_date
FROM injury_phases i
JOIN display_names n ON i.person_id = n.id AND entity_type = 'persons'
AND start_date_time BETWEEN '2007-07-01' AND '2007-07-31'
ORDER BY full_name, injury_type
```

Bold: Indicates a new term, an important word, or words that you see onscreen. For example, words in menus or dialog boxes appear in the text like this. Here is an example: "You can save time by clicking the **Get fields to select** button, which fills the grid with all the incoming fields."

Warnings or important notes appear like this.

Tips and tricks appear like this.

Get in touch

Feedback from our readers is always welcome.

General feedback: Email feedback@packtpub.com and mention the book title in the subject of your message. If you have questions about any aspect of this book, please email us at questions@packtpub.com.

Errata: Although we have taken every care to ensure the accuracy of our content, mistakes do happen. If you have found a mistake in this book, we would be grateful if you would report this to us. Please visit www.packtpub.com/submit-errata, selecting your book, clicking on the Errata Submission Form link, and entering the details.

Piracy: If you come across any illegal copies of our works in any form on the Internet, we would be grateful if you would provide us with the location address or website name. Please contact us at copyright@packtpub.com with a link to the material.

If you are interested in becoming an author: If there is a topic that you have expertise in and you are interested in either writing or contributing to a book, please visit authors.packtpub.com.

Reviews

Please leave a review. Once you have read and used this book, why not leave a review on the site that you purchased it from? Potential readers can then see and use your unbiased opinion to make purchase decisions, we at Packt can understand what you think about our products, and our authors can see your feedback on their book. Thank you!

For more information about Packt, please visit packtpub.com.

Getting Started with PDI

1

Pentaho Data Integration (**PDI**) is a popular business intelligence tool, used for exploring, transforming, validating, and migrating data, along with other useful operations. PDI allows you to perform all of the preceding tasks thanks to its friendly user interface, modern architecture, and rich functionality. This book will introduce you to the tool, giving you a quick understanding of the daily tasks that you can perform with it.

We will cover the following topics in this chapter:

- Introducing PDI
- Installing PDI
- Configuring the graphical designer tool
- Creating a simple transformation
- Understanding the Kettle home directory

Introducing PDI

PDI, also known as **Kettle**, is a very powerful tool. It can be used for performing typical **Extract, Transform, and Load** (ETL) processes. PDI gets data from different sources and manipulates it in many ways (deduplicating, filtering, cleaning, and formatting, among others), saving the data in different formats and destinations. The following diagram illustrates a very simple example of an ETL process designed with PDI:

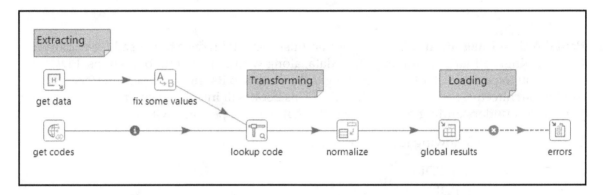

ETL process

Aside from the preceding processes, PDI serves to migrate data between applications, access and manipulate real-time data, access data in the cloud, orchestrate administrative tasks, and more.

Installing PDI

The following are the instructions to install the PDI **Community Edition** (**CE**), irrespective of the operating system that you may be using:

- Make sure that you have JRE 8.0 installed.

If you don't have JRE 8.0 installed, download it from `http://www.jae Redash source code by cloning the repository, anva.com` and install it before proceeding. Make sure that the `JAVA_HOME` system variable is set.

- Go to the download page at: `https://sourceforge.net/projects/pentaho/files/Data%20Integration/`.
- Choose the latest stable release. At the time of writing this book, it is **8.1**, as shown in the following screenshot:

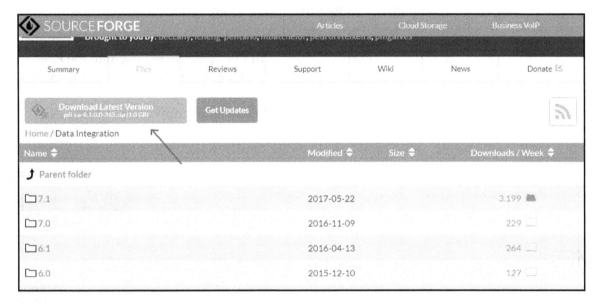

PDI on SourceForge.net

- Download the available ZIP file, which will serve you for all platforms.
- Unzip the downloaded file in a folder of your choice (for example, `c:/software/pdi` or `/home/pdi_user/pdi`).
- Browse your disk and look for the PDI folder that was just created. You will see a folder named `data-integration`, with several subfolders (`lib`, `plugins`, `samples`, and more) and a bunch of scripts (`spoon.bat`, `pan.bat`, and others), which we will soon learn how to use.

Configuring the graphical designer tool

Spoon is PDI's desktop designer tool. With Spoon, you can design, preview, and test all of your work (that is, **transformations** and **jobs**).

Before starting to work with PDI, it's advisable to take a look at the Spoon interface and do some minimal configuration. The instructions are as follows:

- **Start Spoon**: If your system is Windows, run `Spoon.bat` from within the PDI installation directory. On other platforms, such as Unix, Linux, and so on, open a Terminal window and type `spoon.sh`.
- The main window will show up, with a **Welcome!** window already open, as shown in the following screenshot:

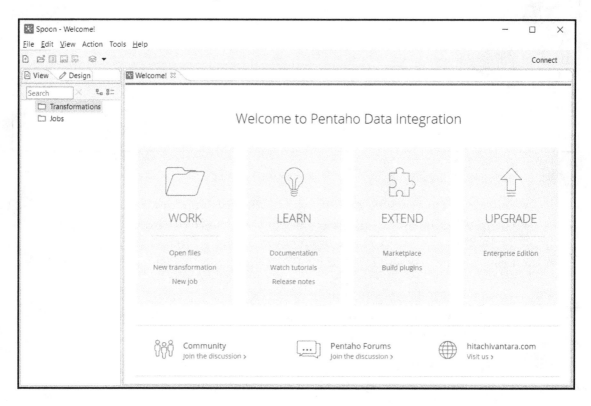

Welcome page

The **Welcome!** page includes some links to web resources, forums, and more, as well as some shortcuts for working with PDI. You can reach that window at any time by navigating to the **Help | Welcome Screen** option.

In order to customize Spoon, do the following:

- Click on **Options...** in the **Tools** menu. A window appears, where you can change various general characteristics, as follows:

Kettle Options	×

General \ Look & Feel

Preview data batch size:	1000
Max number of lines in the logging windows:	5000
Central log line store timeout in minutes:	720
Max number of lines in the log history views:	50
Show welcome page at startup:	☑
Use database cache:	☑
Open last file at startup:	☑
Autosave changed files:	☐
Only show the active file in the main tree:	☑
Only save used connections to XML:	☑
Replace existing objects on open/import:	☑
Ask before replacing objects:	☐
Show Save dialog:	☑
Automatically split hops:	☐
Show Copy or Distribute dialog:	☑
Show repository dialog at startup:	☐
Ask user when exiting:	☐
Clear custom parameters (steps/plugins):	⟲
Auto collapse palette tree:	☑
Display tooltips:	☑
Show help tooltips:	☑

OK   Cancel

Options

- Many of the options in this tab will not make sense to you yet. Instead of doing anything here, select the tab **Look & Feel**:

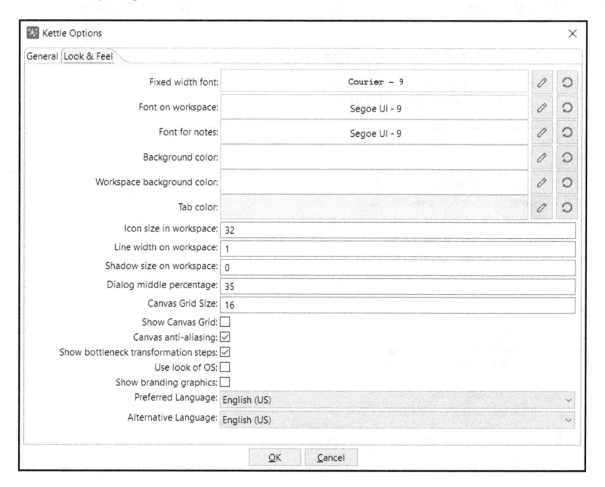

Look & Feel options

- Feel free to change any of the options in this tab (for example, the font color or size). Click on the **OK** button.
- Restart Spoon to apply the changes.

Creating a simple transformation

Transformations and jobs are the main PDI artifacts. Transformations are data-flow oriented entities, while jobs are task-oriented. In this book, we will start by learning all about transformations, focusing on jobs later. To get a quick idea of what, exactly, a transformation is, we will start by creating a simple one. This will also allow you to see what it's like to work with Spoon.

Our first transformation will find out the current version of PDI (Kettle), and will print the value to the log. Proceed as follows:

- On the **Welcome page**, click on the New transformation link, located under the **WORK** link group. Alternatively, press *Ctrl + N*.
- A new tab will appear, with the title Transformation 1. It's in this tab that you will create your work.
- To the left of the screen, under the **Design** tab, you'll see a tree of folders. Expand the Input folder by double-clicking on it.

Note that if you work in macOS, a single click is enough.

- Then, left-click on the **Get System Info** icon, and, without releasing the button, drag and drop the selected icon to the work area (that is, the blank area that occupies almost all of the screen). You should see something like this:

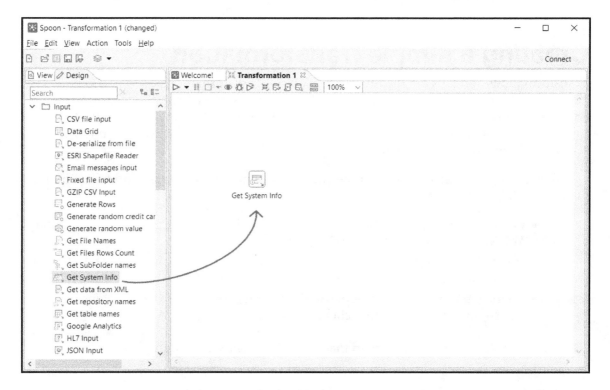

Dragging and dropping a step

- Double-click on the **Get System Info** icon. A configuration window will show up. Fill in the first row in the grid, as shown in the following screenshot. Note that you don't have to type the Kettle version. Instead, you can choose it from a list of available options:

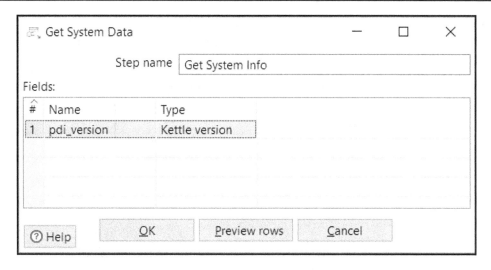

Configuring the Get System Info step

- In the **Design** tab, double-click on the Utility folder, click on the Write to log icon, and drag and drop it to the work area.
- Put the mouse cursor over the **Get System Info** icon and wait until a tiny toolbar shows up, as shown in the following screenshot:

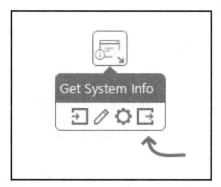

Mouseover assistance toolbar

- Click on the output connector (the icon highlighted in the preceding image) and drag it towards the Write to log icon. A greyed hop is displayed.

- When the mouse cursor is over the **Write to log** step, release the button. A link (a hop, from now on) is created, from the first step to the second one. The screen should look as follows:

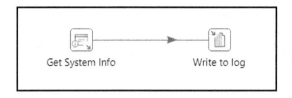

Connecting steps with a hop

Let's add some color note to our work, as follows:

- Right-click anywhere in the work area to bring up a contextual menu.
- In the menu, select the **New Note...** option. A note editor will appear.
- Type a description, such as My first transformation. Select the **Font style** tab and choose a nice font and some colors for your note, and then click on **OK**. The following should be the final result:

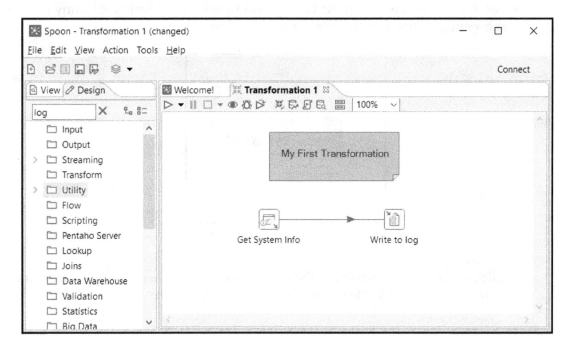

My first transformation

- Save the transformation by pressing *Ctrl + S*. PDI will ask for a destination folder. Select the folder of your choice, and give the transformation a name. PDI will save the transformation as a file with a `ktr` extension (for example, `sample_transformation.ktr`).

Finally, let's run the transformation to see what happens:

- Click on the Run icon, located in the transformation toolbar:

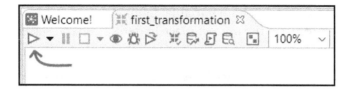

Run icon in the transformation toolbar

- A window named **Run Options** will appear. Click on **Run**.
- At the bottom of the screen, you should see a log with the results of the execution:

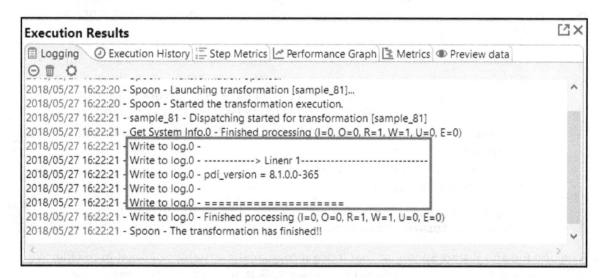

Execution Results

Understanding the Kettle home directory

When you run Spoon for the first time, a folder named .kettle is created in your home directory by default. This folder is referred to as the **Kettle home directory**.

The folder contains several configuration files, mainly created and updated by the different PDI tools. Among these files, there is the kettle.properties file.

The purpose of the kettle.properties file – created along with the .kettle folder, the first time you run Spoon – is to contain variable definitions with a broad scope: Java Virtual Machine. Therefore, it's the perfect place to define general settings; some examples are as follows:

- Database connection settings: host, database name, and so on
- SMTP settings: SMTP server, port, and so on
- Common input and output folders
- Directory to send log files to

Before continuing, let's add some variables to the file. Suppose that you have two folders, named C:/PDI/INPUT and C:/PDI/OUTPUT, which you will use for storing files. The objective will be to add two variables, named INPUT_FOLDER and OUTPUT_FOLDER, containing those values:

1. Locate the Kettle home directory. If you work in Windows, the folder could be C:\Documents and Settings\<your_name> or C:\Users\<your_name>, depending on which Windows version you have. If you work in Linux (or similar) or macOS, the folder will most likely be /home/<your_name>/.
2. Edit the kettle.properties file. You will see that it only contains commented sample lines.
3. You can safely remove the contents of the file and define your own variables by typing the following lines:

```
INPUT_FOLDER=C:/PDI/INPUT
OUTPUT_FOLDER=C:/PDI/OUTPUT
```

Save the file and restart Spoon, so that it can recognize the variables defined in the file. We will learn how to use these variables in Chapter 2, *Getting Familiar with Spoon*.

Summary

In this chapter, you were introduced to Pentaho Data Integration. Specifically, you learned what PDI is, and you installed the tool. You were introduced to Spoon, PDI's graphical designer tool, and you created your first transformation. You were also introduced to the Kettle home directory and the `kettle.properties` file, which will be used throughout the rest of the book.

In `Chapter 2`, *Getting Familiar with Spoon*, you will learn much more about the process of creating, testing, and running transformations in Spoon.

Getting Familiar with Spoon 2

This chapter will show you how to work with Spoon by designing, debugging, and testing a transformation. In addition to exploring Spoon features, you will also learn the basics for handling errors when you are designing a transformation.

This chapter will cover the following topics:

- Exploring the Spoon interface
- Designing, previewing, and running transformations
- Defining and using Kettle variables
- Running transformations with the pan utility

Exploring the Spoon interface

In Chapter 1, *Getting Started with PDI*, you used Spoon to create your first transformation. In this chapter, you will learn more about the experience of working with Spoon. First, let's take a look at its interface. The following screenshot shows you the different areas, menus, and toolboxes present in Spoon:

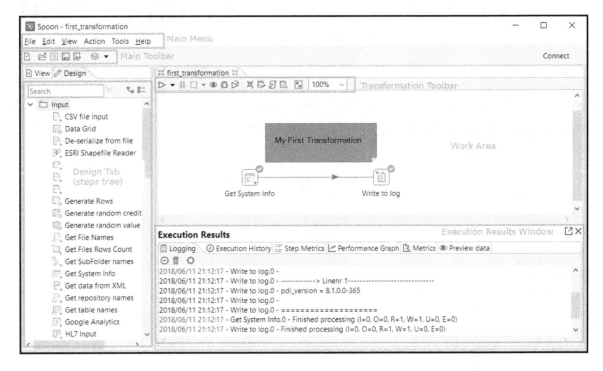

Spoon interface

The following provides a brief description of every component shown in the preceding screenshot:

- **Main Menu**: This menu includes general options, such as opening and saving files (namely, transformations and jobs), editing and searching features, configuration settings, and help options.

Most of the options in the main menu contain shortcuts that you can memorize and use, if you prefer to do so.

- **Main Toolbar**: This toolbar serves as an alternative way to create, open, and save files.
- **Transformation Toolbar**: This toolbar contains options for running, previewing, and validating the open transformation.
- **Work Area**: This is the area where you create your work.
- **Design and View Tabs**: When you have a transformation open in the main area, the **Design** tab shows a tree with all of the steps available to add to the transformation. If you click on top of the **View** tab, you will see a tree with all of the elements added to the transformation so far (database connections, steps, hops, and more):

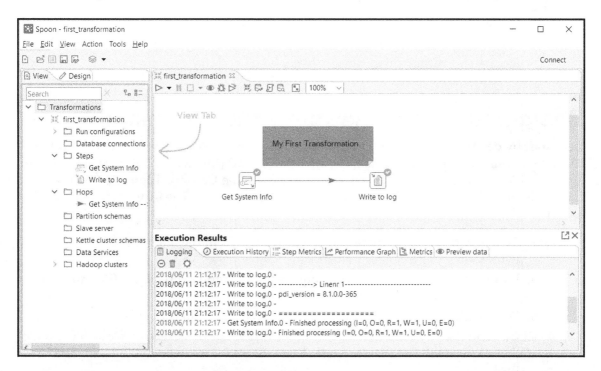

View tab in Spoon

- **Execution Results**: As the name implies, in this window, you see the results of previewing or executing a transformation or a job. You already know the first tab, **Logging**, where the details of the current execution are displayed.

Now that you know the names and contents of the different components in Spoon, it will be easier to work on the next sections.

Designing, previewing, and running transformations

In this section, we will create a transformation that is a bit more interesting than the one you already built. In doing this, you will have a chance to learn about the process of designing transformations, while also previewing your work.

The task is as follows: you will be given a file with a list of cities in the USA, along with their zip codes and their state names. You will have to generate a file containing only the cities in the state of NY, sorted by zip code. We will split the task into the following steps:

- Designing and previewing the transformation
- Learning to deal with errors that may appear
- Saving and running the transformation

Designing and previewing a transformation

Let's start by developing the first part of the transformation. We will read the file and filter the data. In this case, the solution is quite straightforward (this will not always be the case). There is a PDI step for each of the tasks to accomplish. The **CSV file input** step will serve for reading the file, and the **Filter rows** step will filter the rows. The instructions are as follows:

1. First, create a transformation. You can do this from the main menu, from the main toolbar, or by pressing *Ctrl + T*.
2. From the `Input` folder that contains steps, drag and drop a **CSV file input** step to the work area.
3. Double-click on the step. A configuration window will show up.
4. Click on the **Browse...** button to locate the file. For this exercise, we will use a file that comes with the PDI software. You will find it in the following path, under the installation folder: `samples\transformations\files\Zipssortedbycityst ate.csv`.
5. Click on **Get Fields**. The grid will be filled with the columns found in the file:

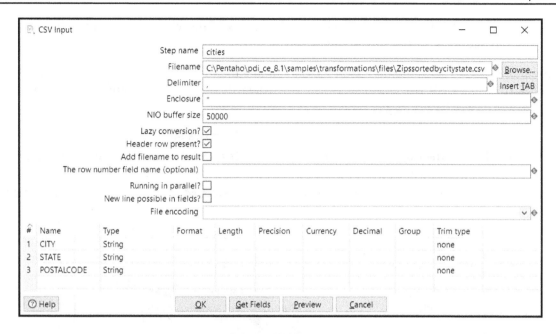

Configuring a CSV file input step

6. Click on **Preview**, then click on **OK**. A window with sample data will appear, as shown in the following screenshot:

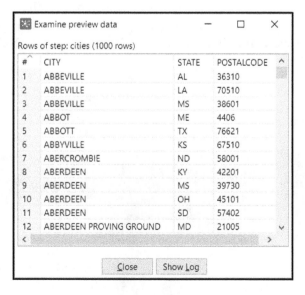

Sample data

7. Click on **Close** to close the **Examine preview data** window, and then click on **OK** to close the configuration window.

Now that we have read the file, the data is available for further processing. The rows coming from the **CSV file input** step will flow towards the next step, which will be the filter:

- From the Flow folder, drag and drop a **Filter rows** step.
- Click on the output connector in the **CSV file input** step to create a hop towards the **Filter rows** step.
- You will be prompted for the kind of hop. Select **Main output of step**, shown as follows:

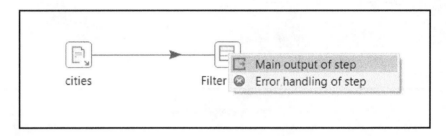

Selecting a kind of hop

- Double-click on the **Filter rows** step to configure the filter.
- Fill in the configuration window, as shown in the following screenshot, to indicate that we will only keep rows with states equal to **NY**:

Configuring a filter

- Close the window. The following is what you should have so far:

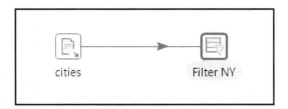

Simple transformation

Now, we will preview the results to see if we get what we expected:

1. Make sure that the **Filter rows** step is selected.

 When a step is selected, its border becomes wider, as shown in the previous screenshot.

2. Press *F10* to preview the results. Alternatively, click on the Preview icon (the icon that looks like an eye) in the transformation toolbar. Then, click on **Quick Launch**. A window with the filtered rows will appear, as follows:

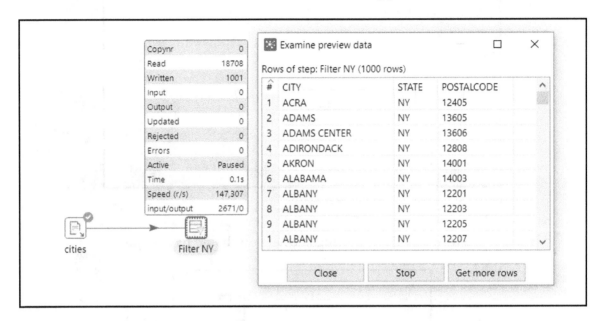

Previewing data

By default, only 1,000 rows are previewed. If you want to look at more data, just click on **Get more rows**.

3. Click on **Stop** to stop the previewing process and close the window.

As you can see in the preceding image, when you preview or run a transformation, a small window with metrics is displayed above the steps while the rows are being processed. These metrics are the same as those shown in the **Steps metrics** tab in the **Execution Results** window.

Understanding the logging options

PDI logs all of the executions of a transformation. By default, the level of the logging details is basic, but there are seven possible levels of logging, ranging from **Nothing at all** to **Rowlevel (very detailed)**, which is the most detailed level of logging. You can change the level of logging as follows:

- If you will run a transformation, in the **Execute a transformation** window, before clicking on **Run**, select the proper option:

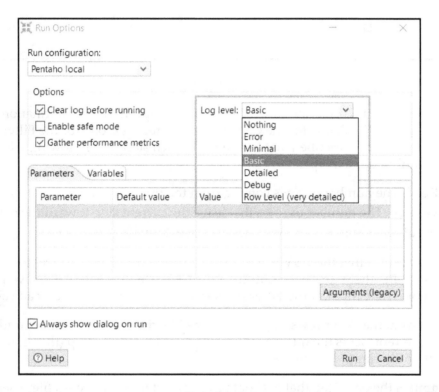

Selecting the Log level

- If you are previewing a transformation, instead of clicking on **Quick Launch**, select **Configure**. This will show you the **Execute a transformation** window. In this window, choose **Log level**, and then click on **Run**.

Understanding the Step Metrics tab

Before continuing, let's observe what is happening in the **Execution Results** window. You already know the **Logging** tab, which displays every task that you are performing. Now, click on the **Step Metrics** tab. You will see the following:

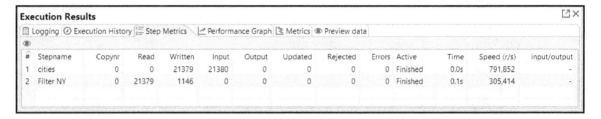

Step Metrics tab

In this tab, there is a grid with one row for each of the steps in the transformation. In this case, we have two of them: one for the **CSV file input** step, and one for the **Filter rows** step. The columns in the grid describe what happened in each step. The following are the most relevant columns in our example:

- **Read**: The number of rows coming from the previous step
- **Written**: The number of rows that leave the current step toward the next one
- **Input**: The number of rows coming from external sources

For instance, the rows that the **CSV file input** step reads from the file travel toward the **Filter rows** step. In other words, the output of the **CSV file input** step, displayed under the **Written** column, is the input of the **Filter rows** step, displayed under the **Read** column.

Also, if you look at the **Filter rows** line in the **Steps Metrics** grid, the number under the **Written** column represents the number of rows that will leave the step (that is, the rows remaining after filtering).

CSV file input is the only step that gets data from an external source – a file. Therefore, this is the only step that has a value greater than zero in the **Input** column.

The last columns in the grid – **Time**, **Speed (r/s)**, and **input/output** – are metrics to monitor the performance of the execution. As to the rest of the columns in the grid, they will be described in later chapters.

Dealing with errors while designing

Now, we will continue working on the transformation created in the previous section. This time, we will sort the final data by ZIP code. This is a very simple task, but we will use it as a method to learn how to deal with errors that may appear while we are designing:

1. From the `Transform` folder that contains steps, drag and drop a **Sort rows** step to the work area.

2. Create a hop from the **Filter rows** step to this one. Again, you will be prompted for the kind of hop. Select the **Main output of step** option:

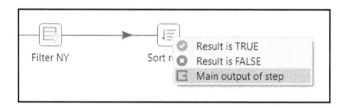

Kinds of hop leaving a Filter rows step

3. Double-click on the Sort rows icon. Fill in the grid as follows:

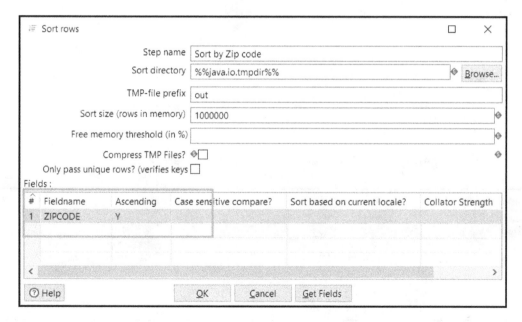

Sorting data

4. Close the window.
5. Make sure that the Sort rows step is selected, and run a preview like you did before. If you followed the steps as explained, you will get an error.

There are several indications that will help you to understand that an error occurred:

- A small red icon will appear in the upper-right corner of one or more steps. These are the steps that are causing the error.
- The backgrounds of the corresponding rows in the **Step Metrics** tab will change to red:

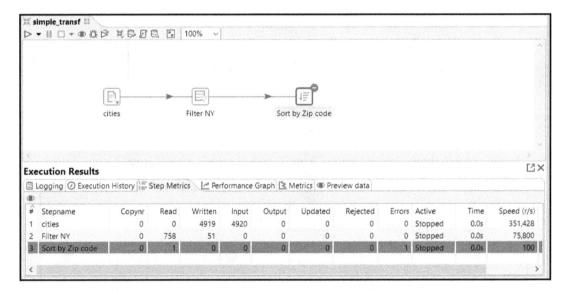

Errors in the Step Metrics tab

- The **Logging** tab will contain text explaining the error:

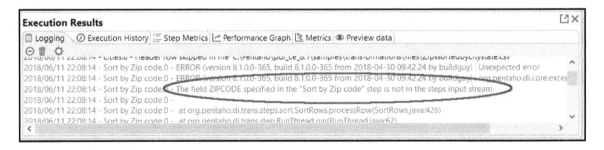

Errors in the Logging tab

In this case, as stated in the log, the problem was that we were referring to a field that doesn't exist. We typed ZIPCODE instead of POSTALCODE. Let's fix it, as follows:

1. Double-click on the **Sort rows** step and fix the name of the field
2. Close the window and run a preview again
3. You will see the rows with states equal to NY, sorted by ZIP code

Saving and running a transformation

The last task before saving and running the transformation is to send the results to a file. This is quite easy:

1. From the Output folder, drag and drop a **Text file output** step to the work area. Create a hop from the **Sort rows** step to this new step. Note that this time, you don't have to choose the kind of hop; a default kind of hop will be created.
2. Double-click on the **Text file output** step. In the configuration window, provide a name for the file that we will generate. You should specify the full path, for instance, C:/Pentaho/data/ny_cities.

 You don't have to type the extension; it is automatically added, as indicated in the **extension** textbox.

3. Close the window.

The transformation is complete. The only task to perform now is to save it and run it, as follows:

1. Save the transformation. You can do so by pressing *Ctrl + S* or by selecting the proper option from **Main Menu** or **Main Toolbar**.

2. Once the transformation has saved, you can run it. Do so by pressing *F9*. In the **Logging** tab of the **Execution Results** window, you will see the log of the execution. If you select the **Preview data** tab in the same window, you will see sample data coming from the step currently selected. As an example, click on the **Filter rows** step and look at the data in the **Preview data** tab. You will see all of the rows for the state of NY, although they are still out of order:

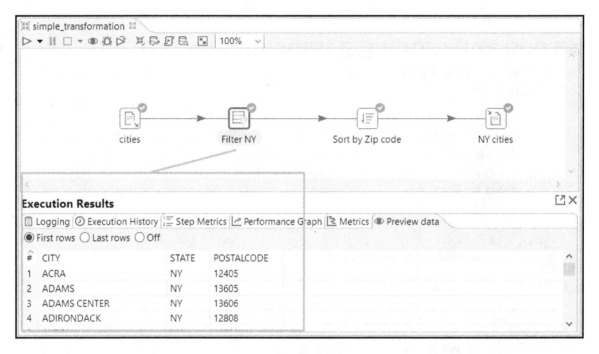

Preview data tab

3. If you click on the Sort rows step, you will see the same, but ordered. Also, a file should have been created with the same information. Browse your system to look for the generated file. Its content should be something like the following:

```
CITY;STATE;POSTALCODE
 NEW YORK;NY;10001
 NEW YORK;NY;10003
 NEW YORK;NY;10005
 . . .
 . . .
 ELMIRA;NY;14925
 HOLTSVILLE;NY;501
 FISHERS ISLAND;NY;6390
```

If you look at the sample lines, you will note that the code 501 is between 14925 and 6390. The codes are not sorted by number, but alphabetically. This is because the ZIP code was defined as a String in the input step.

Defining and using Kettle variables

In PDI, you can define and use variables, just as you do when you code in any computer language. We already defined a couple of variables when we created the kettle.properties file in Chapter 1, *Getting Started with PDI*. Now, we will see where and how to use them.

It's simple: any time you see a dollar sign by the side of a textbox, you can use a variable:

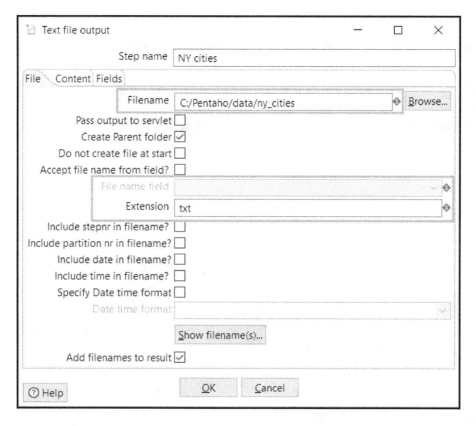

Sample textboxes that allow variables

You can reference a variable by enclosing its name in curly braces, preceded by a dollar sign (for example, `${INPUT_FOLDER}`).

A less used notation for a variable is as follows: `%%<variable name>%%` (for example, `%%INPUT_FOLDER%%`).

Let's go back to the transformation created in the previous section. Instead of a fixed value for the location of the output file, we will use variables. The following describes how to do it:

1. Open the transformation (if you had closed it). You can do this from **Main Menu** or from **Main Toolbar**.
2. Double-click on the **Text file output** step. Replace the full path for the location of the file with the following: `${OUTPUT_FOLDER}/${FILENAME}`.

Note that you can combine variables, and can also mix variable names with static text.

3. Close the window and press *F10* to run the transformation.

4. In the window that appears, select the **Variables** tab. You will see the names of both variables – OUTPUT_FOLDER and FILENAME:

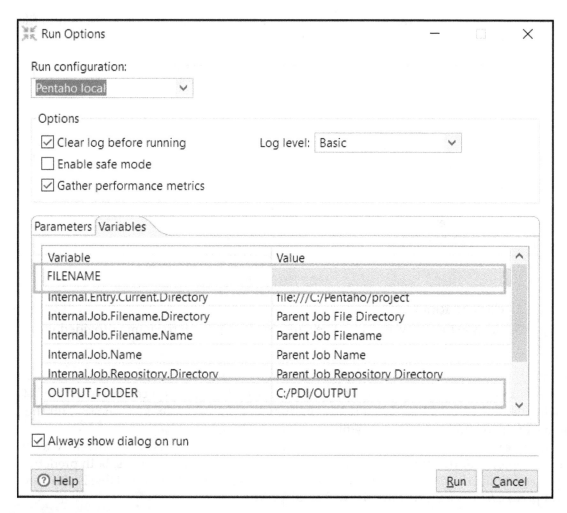

Variables in the Execute a Transformation window

The OUTPUT_FOLDER variable already has a value, which is taken from the kettle.properties file. The FILENAME variable doesn't have a value yet.

1. To the right of the name, type the name that you want to give to the output file, as shown in the following screenshot:

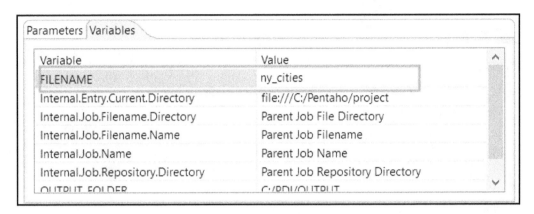

Variable	Value
FILENAME	ny_cities
Internal.Entry.Current.Directory	file:///C:/Pentaho/project
Internal.Job.Filename.Directory	Parent Job File Directory
Internal.Job.Filename.Name	Parent Job Filename
Internal.Job.Name	Parent Job Name
Internal.Job.Repository.Directory	Parent Job Repository Directory
OUTPUT FOLDER	C:/PDI/OUTPUT

Entering values for variables

2. Click on **Run**
3. Browse the filesystem to make sure that the file with the name provided was generated

Beside the user-defined variables – those created by you, either in the kettle.properties file or inside Spoon – PDI has a list of predefined variables that you can also use. The list mainly includes variables related to the environment (for example, ${os.name}, for the name of the operating system on which you are working, or ${Internal.Entry.Current.Directory}, which references the file directory where the current job or transformation is saved). To see the full list of variables, both predefined and user-defined, just position the cursor inside any textbox where a variable is allowed, and press *Ctrl + Spacebar*. A full list will be displayed.

- If you click on any of the variables for a second, the actual value of the variable will be shown, as indicated in the following screenshot:

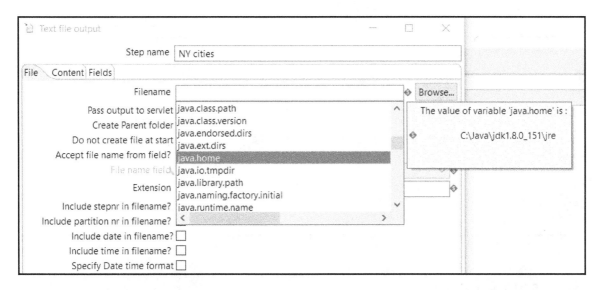

PDI variables

- If you double-click on a variable name, the name will be transcribed into the textbox.

Using named parameters

In the last exercise, you used two variables: one created in the `kettle.properties` file, and the other created inside of Spoon at runtime. There are still more ways to define variables. One of them is to create a *named parameter*. Named parameters are variables that you define in a transformation, and they can have a default value. You only have to supply a value if it differs from the default. Let's look at how it works, as follows:

1. Open the last transformation (if you had closed it).
2. Double-click anywhere in the work area excepting over the steps or hops. This will open the **Transformation properties** window.

3. Click on the **Variables** tab. This is where we define the named parameters.

4. Fill in the grid as shown, replacing the path in the example with the real path where you have PDI installed:

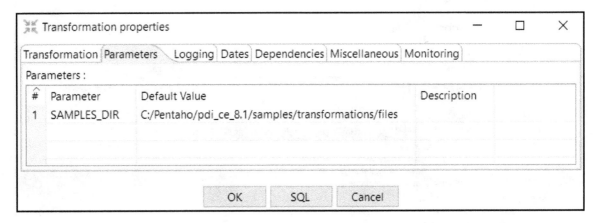

Defining a named parameter

5. Close the window.

6. Double-click on the **CSV file input** step. Replace the full path of the location of the file with the following: `${SAMPLES_DIR}/Zipssortedbycitystate.csv`.

7. Close the window and save the transformation.

8. Click *F9* to run the transformation. The **Parameters** tab in the **Run Options** window will show the named parameter that we just defined:

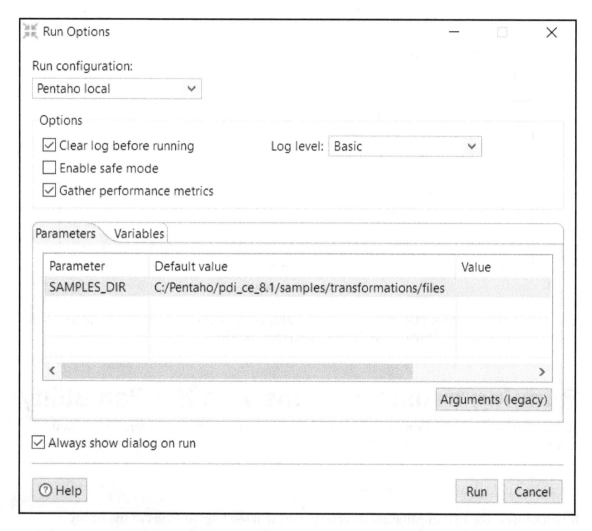

Running a transformation with a named parameter

9. Click on **Run**. PDI will replace the value of the variable, exactly as it did before.

Note that this time, we didn't supply a value for the variable, as it already had a proper value. Now, suppose that we move the samples folder to a different location. The following describes how we can provide the new value:

- Click *F9* to run the transformation.
- In the **Parameters** tab, fill in the **Value** column with the proper value, as shown in the following screenshot:

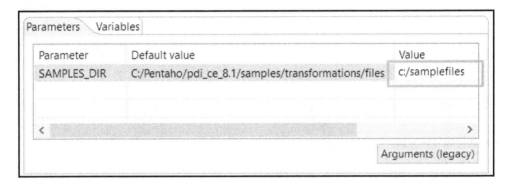

Supplying a value for a named parameter

- Click on **Run**. PDI will replace the value of the variable with the value that you provided, and will read the file from that location.

Running transformations with the Pan utility

So far, you have used Spoon to create and run transformations. However, if you want to run a transformation in a production environment, you won't use Spoon, but a command-line utility named `Pan`.

Let's quickly look at how to use this tool.

If you browse the PDI installation directory, you will see two versions of the utility: `Pan.bat` and `Pan.sh`. You will use the first if you have a Windows environment, and the second for other systems.

In the next step-by-step tutorial, we will assume that you have Windows, but you should make the required adjustments if you have a different system.

The simplest way to run a transformation with `Pan` is to provide the full path of the transformation that you want to run. You can execute `Pan` in Windows as follows:

```
Pan.bat /file=<ktr file name>
```

For Unix, Linux, and other Unix-like systems, use the following command:

```
./Pan.sh /file=<ktr file name>
```

Let's suppose that you want to run the first transformation created in this chapter, which is located in the following directory:

```
c:/pdi_labs/my_first_transformation.ktr
```

In order to run it, follow these instructions:

1. Open a Terminal window
2. Go to the directory where PDI is installed and type the following code:

   ```
   Pan /file=c:/pdi_labs/my_first_transformation.ktr
   ```

 You must include the full path for the transformation file. If the name contains spaces, surround it with double quotes.

After running the command, you will see the log of the execution, which is the same log that you see in the **Execution Results** window in Spoon. In order to change the `log level`, just add the following:

```
-level:<log level>
```

The possible values for the log level are `Nothing`, `Minimal`, `Error`, `Basic`, `Detailed`, `Debug`, and `Rowlevel`.

As an example, the following command will print not only the basic log, but also the details of every row that is being processed:

```
Pan - level:Rowlevel /file=c:/pdi_labs/my_first_transformation.ktr
```

The details of the rows are as follows:

```
...
2018/06/10 12:33:43 - Sort rows.0 - Read row: [YONKERS], [NY], [10701]
2018/06/10 12:33:43 - Sort rows.0 - Read row: [YONKERS], [NY], [10703]
2018/06/10 12:33:43 - Sort rows.0 - Read row: [YONKERS], [NY], [10705]
2018/06/10 12:33:43 - Sort rows.0 - Read row: [YORKVILLE], [NY], [13495]
2018/06/10 12:33:43 - Sort rows.0 - Read row: [YULAN], [NY], [12792]
2018/06/10 12:33:43 - Sort rows.0 - Signaling 'output done' to 0 output
rowsets.
2018/06/10 12:33:43 - Sort rows.0 - Finished processing (I=0, O=0, R=1146,
W=1146, U=0, E=0)
```

In the last version of our transformation, we added a named parameter with the path where PDI had to look for the input file. In Spoon, you provided the value in the **Execution** window. When running the transformation with `Pan`, you do it by using the `param` option, as follows:

```
/param:<parameter name>=<parameter value>
```

In our example, supposing that the new value is `c:/samples`, we build the command-line parameter as follows:

```
/param:"NAME=c:/samples"
```

> If you want to know all of the possible options for the `Pan` command, run `Pan.bat` or `Pan.sh` without parameters, and all of the options will be displayed.

Summary

This chapter served to help you get used to Spoon, the PDI graphical designer. First, you learned how to work with the tool when you created, previewed, and ran transformations. When you worked with transformations, you had the opportunity to use Kettle variables, both predefined and user defined. You also learned how to deal with common errors. Finally, you experimented with the Pan utility, which is used for running transformations from the command line.

Now that you have seen an overview of the tool, you're ready to get into the details of extracting data. That will be the subject of `Chapter 3`, *Extracting Data*.

Extracting Data 3

Extracting data is all about getting and combining data from different sources, before transforming it in different ways. PDI offers connectivity to a big list of data sources, including all kinds of databases, both commercial and open source. It can also connect to a wide variety of files, both structured and unstructured. The list includes CSV files, properties files, fixed-width text files, and proprietary formats. In particular, this chapter will explain how to get data from plain files and relational databases.

The following topics will be covered in this chapter:

- Getting data from plain files
- Getting data from relational databases
- Getting data from other sources
- Combining different sources into a single dataset

Getting data from plain files

In this section, you will learn how to get data from plain files (for example, `.txt` and CSV files). We will start by explaining how to read and configure such files, and then we will explain how PDI allows you to read multiple files at once, compressed files, and files stored in remote locations.

Reading plain files

In the previous chapter, we experimented with reading a simple file, but this time we will go into detail on getting and properly configuring a simple file's metadata.

 For this and some of the future exercises in this book, we will use `.csv` files with surveys of the Airbnb website. The sample data can be downloaded from `http://tomslee.net/airbnb-data-collection-get-the-data`.

For this exercise, we will read and configure a file with data about a survey carried out in Amsterdam. The file looks as follows:

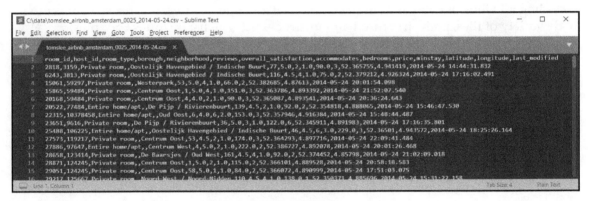

Sample file

This time, we will use a **Text file input** step, which is much more flexible than the **CSV file input** that you are familiar with:

1. Create a new transformation.
2. From the **Input** category of steps, drag and drop a **Text file input** step into the work area.

3. Double-click on the step.

4. In the configuration window, click on the **Browse...** button and locate the file to read. In our example, the file is `tomslee_airbnb_amsterdam_0025_2014-05-24.csv`.

5. After selecting the file, click on **Add**. The full path for the file will be moved from the **File or directory** textbox to the lower grid, as shown in the following screenshot:

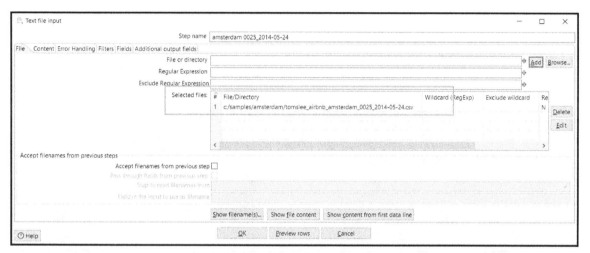

Specifying a file to read with the Text file input step

Feel free to replace any part of the full name with variable names, as you learned how to do in the `Chapter 02`, *Getting Familiar with Spoon.*

6. Click on the **Content** tab. As shown in the following screenshot, PDI assumes that the separator will be a comma (,), and that the file will have a single line as a header. So, in this case, we don't have to modify anything on the screen:

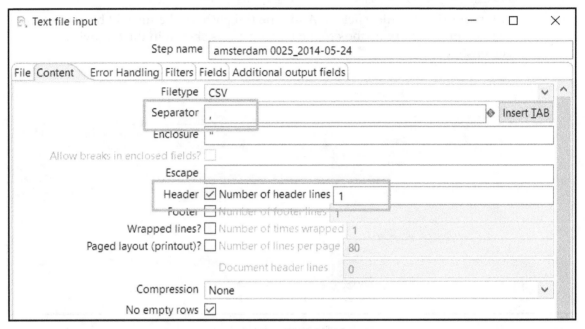

Configuring the contents of a file

7. Now, select the **Fields** tab. This is where we define the fields coming from the file, along with its metadata.
8. Click on **Get Fields**. A small window will ask for the number of sample lines.
9. Click on **OK**, so that PDI guesses the metadata (the type and format of each field) based on the sample lines.

10. A **Scan results** window will appear. Close it. You will see how the grid was populated with all of the fields, data types, and masks, according to what PDI inferred:

#	Name	Type	Format	Position	Length	Precision
1	room_id	Integer	#		15	0
2	host_id	Integer	#		15	0
3	room_type	String			15	
4	borough	String			0	
5	neighborhood	String			38	
6	reviews	Integer	#		15	0
7	overall_satisfaction	Number	#.#		3	1
8	accommodates	Integer	#		15	0
9	bedrooms	Number	#.#		3	1
1	price	Number	#.#		5	1
1	minstay	Integer	#		15	0
1	latitude	Number	#.#		9	6
1	longitude	Number	#.#		8	6
1	last_modified	Date	yyyy-MM-dd HH:mm:ss.SSS			

Grid with fields

If, in the windows asking for the sample lines, we had clicked on **Cancel** instead, all of the fields would have been defined as String.

Whether it was the PDI or you that populated the grid, you can still do the necessary fixes. For example, for the `bedroom` field, PDI assigned the `Number` type. You can safely change it to `Integer`, as well as replace the mask with a #, which represents a number with no decimal places. Also, you can rename a column if you don't like the name in the file. This will not affect the result. The following screenshot shows some possible changes that you could apply to this sample file configuration:

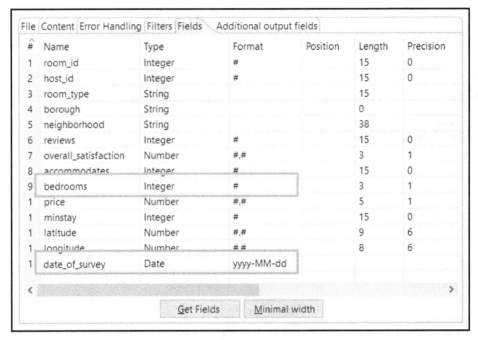

Grid with fields modified manually

Now, it's recommended that you perform a final check, to see if the data has been properly configured:

- Click on **Preview rows**, and then click on **OK**. A window will appear with the first rows in the file, formatted as indicated in the **Fields** grid:

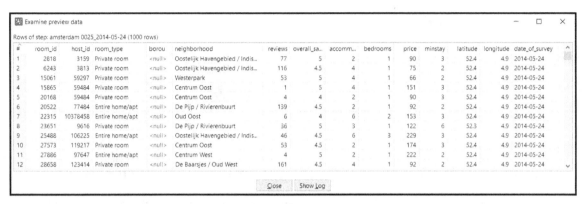

#	room_id	host_id	room_type	borou	neighborhood	reviews	overall_sa...	accomm...	bedrooms	price	minstay	latitude	longitude	date_of_survey
1	2818	3159	Private room	<null>	Oostelijk Havengebied / Indis...	77	5	2	1	90	3	52.4	4.9	2014-05-24
2	6243	3813	Private room	<null>	Oostelijk Havengebied / Indis...	116	4.5	4	1	75	2	52.4	4.9	2014-05-24
3	15061	59297	Private room	<null>	Westerpark	53	5	4	1	66	2	52.4	4.9	2014-05-24
4	15865	59484	Private room	<null>	Centrum Oost	1	5	4	1	151	3	52.4	4.9	2014-05-24
5	20168	59484	Private room	<null>	Centrum Oost	4	4	2	1	90	3	52.4	4.9	2014-05-24
6	20522	77484	Entire home/apt	<null>	De Pijp / Rivierenbuurt	139	4.5	2	1	92	2	52.4	4.9	2014-05-24
7	22315	10378458	Entire home/apt	<null>	Oud Oost	6	4	6	2	153	3	52.4	4.9	2014-05-24
8	23651	9616	Private room	<null>	De Pijp / Rivierenbuurt	36	5	3	1	122	6	52.3	4.9	2014-05-24
9	25488	106225	Entire home/apt	<null>	Oostelijk Havengebied / Indis...	46	4.5	6	3	229	3	52.4	4.9	2014-05-24
10	27573	119217	Private room	<null>	Centrum Oost	53	4.5	2	1	174	3	52.4	4.9	2014-05-24
11	27886	97647	Entire home/apt	<null>	Centrum West	4	5	2	1	222	2	52.4	4.9	2014-05-24
12	28658	123414	Private room	<null>	De Baarsjes / Oud West	161	4.5	4	1	92	2	52.4	4.9	2014-05-24

Previewing rows

In the tutorial, we used the **Text file input** step, which allows us to read plain text files. For reading other kinds of files (for example, Excel files or Properties files), there are dedicated steps. You will not find it difficult to configure them, as they share many configuration settings with the step we used.

Reading files with great versatility

In the previous tutorial, you read a single file. The **Text file input** step allows you to read more than one file at the same time, as long as the files share the same format. Suppose that you want to read all of the files with the surveys carried out in 2015. There are three of them in our set of files, as follows:

```
tomslee_airbnb_amsterdam_0080_2015-01-19.csv
tomslee_airbnb_amsterdam_0106_2015-03-17.csv
tomslee_airbnb_amsterdam_0244_2015-12-16.csv
```

We can read them by typing their full paths into the **Selected files** grid, one file per row, as shown in the following screenshot:

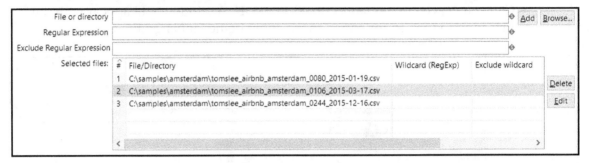

Reading several files at the same time

As an alternative, because the names of the files follow a pattern, instead of typing all of the names, we could decide to write a regular expression that matches all of the filenames.

In any case, to make sure that PDI is reading the files that we expect, we can click on **Show filename(s)...**, and a window will appear with the full list of files that will be read:

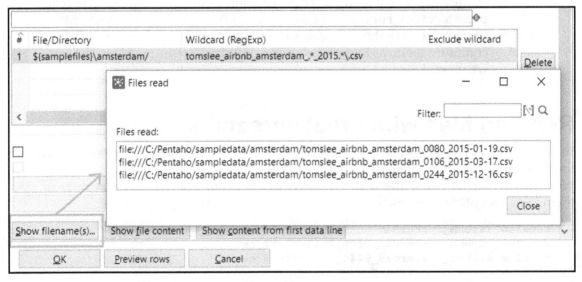

List of files that match a regular expression

You can also read compressed files. The files that we have been using were downloaded in a ZIP format, and you can read the files without unzipping the original. For example, suppose that you want to read the file in the first transformation without extracting the files from the `.zip` file.

You can type `zip:c:\samples\amsterdam.zip!s3_files\amsterdam\tomslee_airbnb_amst erdam_0025_2014-05-24.csv` as the name of the file. In general, the syntax for reading a particular file compressed as a ZIP file is `zip:<compressed file>!<file name>`, where `<compressed file>` is the full path for the `.zip` file and `<file name>` is the name of the file to read, including the path inside the ZIP file.

Reading files from remote locations

PDI uses the **Virtual File System** (**VFS**), which allows you to connect to a variety of filesystems—for example, **Amazon S3**, **HDFS**, or **Google Cloud Storage**. In particular, when specifying a VFS URL instead of the traditional notation, you can refer to both local and remote files, which can also be stored in a compressed format, as shown in the example in the last section. In particular, starting with PDI 8.1, you can read content from Google Drive, which will be explained in the next section.

Reading files from Google Drive

Reading files from **Google Drive** is very simple, but it requires some configuration the first time you try it.

First of all, you have to enable the Google Drive API and generate the credentials that will allow PDI to access the resources on the Drive:

1. Enable the Google Drive API from `https://console.developers.google.com/apis/api/drive.googleapis.com/`.

2. While logged in to the Google platform, create a service account. You can do so by navigating to **Navigation menu** | **IAM & admin** | **Service accounts**:

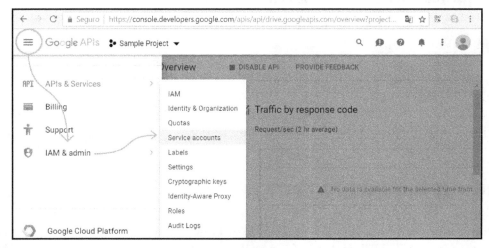

Creating an account

3. Now, generate the credentials. You can do so by navigating to **APIs & Services** | **Credentials** | **Create credentials** and selecting **OAuth client ID**:

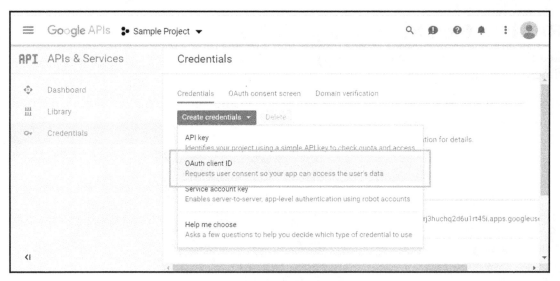

Generating credentials

4. After a few clicks, you will be finished, as shown in the following screenshot:

Google service account

5. Now, click on the highlighted icon to download the credentials in a JSON format. Rename the generated file to `client_secret.json` and copy it into the following folder, inside of the PDI installation location: `/plugins/pentaho-googledrive-vfs/credentials`.

6. In order to recognize the file, you will have to restart Spoon.

Now, suppose that you want to read a file named `listings.csv`, saved in a folder named `pentaho_samples` in your Google Drive. The following describes how to do it:

1. Create a transformation and drag a **Text file input** step to the canvas

2. As the filename, type `googledrive://pentaho_samples/listings.csv`

> In general, for reading a file saved in Google Drive, you specify its name as `googledrive://<filename>`, where the name of the file includes the full path in the drive.

3. After the first attempt to access the file (for example, by clicking on **Show file content**), you will be prompted to log in to your Google account and allow PDI to access the drive.

> After doing this, PDI will store a security token called `StoredCredential` in the same folder where you have saved the credentials. This will allow you to connect later, without authenticating again.

4. Once you have granted PDI access to your drive, you can configure the step for reading the file located in the drive in the same way that you do so when reading local files.

Getting data from relational databases

Relational databases are some of the most common sources of data in any ETL process. PDI enables you to connect and get data from multiple RDBMS engines, including the most popular (for example, Oracle or MySQL) but also other engines. The only prerequisite is that there exists the proper JDBC driver. In this section, you will learn how to connect to, explore, and get data from a database.

Connecting to a database and using the database explorer

There are two things that you must do in order to connect to a database, if you intend to use its data inside PDI:

- Install the proper JDBC driver
- Create a connection to the database

For demonstration purposes, we will connect to a **PostgreSQL** engine where we have installed a sports database, available for download at http://www.sportsdb.org/sd that you have a JDBC drive/samples.

Make sure that you have a JDBC driver, a .jar file – for the engine. Once you have it, you will have to copy it into the lib folder in the PDI installation directory and restart Spoon.

PDI 8.1 comes with a driver for PostgreSQL, but this is not the case for all of the engines, so make sure that you get the proper driver for your engine.

The installation of the driver only has to be done once in your environment. Now that you have the driver installed, you can create a connection to the database, as follows:

1. Create a new transformation.
2. Click on the **View** tab, right-click on the **Database connections** option, and select **New**. A **Database Connection** window will appear.
3. Under **Connection type:**, choose the engine that matches yours. Fill in the textboxes in the **Settings** area with the correspondent values: **Host Name**, **Database Name**, **Port Number**, **Username**, and **Password**. As an example, look at the following database connection, which is configured for the sports database, hosted on a PostgreSQL database in the local machine:

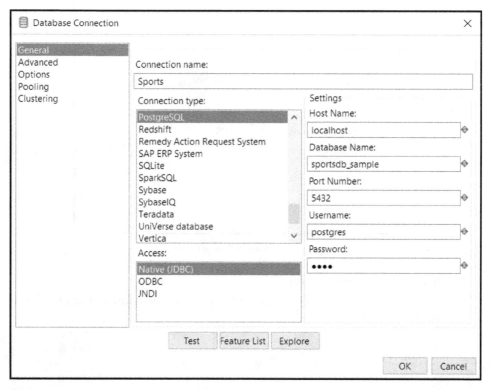

Defining a database connection

 Depending on the type of database, you can choose access methods other than Native (JDBC). Other options include ODBC, JNDI, and OCI.

4. Click on **Test** to verify that the connection is well defined, and that you can reach your database from PDI.

5. Click on **Explore**. The **Database Explorer** will show up.

6. The **Database Explorer** allows you to explore the tables and views in the database, and to run queries and DDL statements.

7. Right-click on the name of any table. A pop-up menu will show up, offering you several options, as shown in the following screenshot:

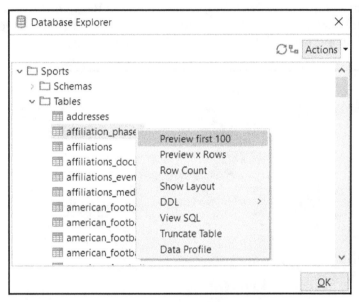

Exploring a table with the Database Explorer

8. Close the **Database Explorer**.

9. Click on **OK**. A new database connection will appear under the **Database connections** item.

You can reach the **Database Explorer** any time you want to, from either **Main Menu** or the **View** tab.

The database connection that you just defined will be available in the current transformation, as you will see shortly. If you want it to be available in new transformations, you have to share it, as follows:

10. Right-click on the database connection and click on **Share**. The name of the connection will become bold, meaning that the definition will be available outside the scope of the current transformation:

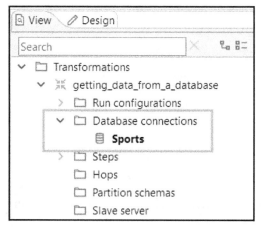

Shared connection

The information about shared database connections is saved in the `shared.xml` file, inside of the **Kettle** home directory.

Getting data from a database

Now that you have defined a connection to a database, you can get data from it. The following describes how to do so:

1. From the `Input` folder, drag and drop a **Table input** step.
2. Double-click on the step to configure it. You will see that a connection is already selected.

> The connection is selected because it is the only database connection that we have created. If there is more than one, you should display the drop-down list and select the connection that you intend to use.

3. Now, use the **SQL** area to write an SQL query. In this case, we will type a query that lists people, along with injuries that they had in July 2007:

```
SELECT full_name
     , injury_type
     , to_char(start_date_time, 'yyyy-mm-dd') as injury_date
FROM injury_phases i
JOIN display_names n ON i.person_id = n.id AND entity_type =
'persons'
 AND start_date_time BETWEEN '2007-07-01' AND '2007-07-31'
ORDER BY full_name, injury_type
```

4. Click on **Preview**, and then click on **OK**. A preview window will appear with sample rows - the results of running the query:

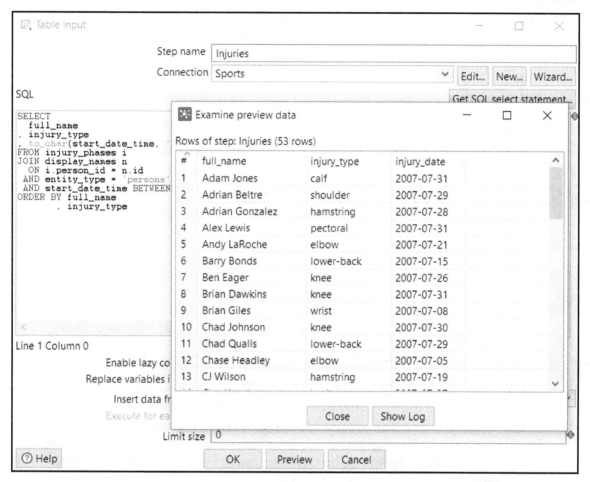

Sample data from a database

5. Close the preview window, and click on **OK** to close the **Table input** step.

6. With the step selected, press *Ctrl + Spacebar* to inspect the output metadata. You will see how PDI translates the database data types into its own types:

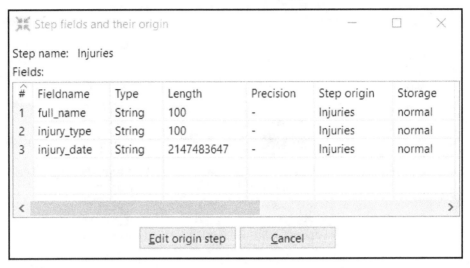

Sample metadata

We will highlight some features of the **Table input** step, as follows:

- You can type any SQL statement, ranging from a simple `select * from table` query to more complex queries, like the one in the example.
- It's recommended that you use ANSI SQL, but you can type any query with a syntax valid in the engine that is being used. For example, `to_char()` function is perfectly valid in PostgreSQL, but it may cause a syntax error in a different engine.
- If `SELECT` contains several fields from a table, you can use **Get SQL select statement...** as a shortcut. This will help you to avoid typing all of the fields manually.

Finally, it's worth noting that in a single transformation, you are not limited to running a single query. You can have more than one **Table input** step, and those steps can run queries connected to different databases.

Aside from RDDMS engines, PDI can connect to and get data from column stores (for example, Cassandra and HBase) and from document stores (for example, MongoDB). These sources have their particularities, and therefore there are separate steps for connecting to them. You can find the corresponding steps inside the `Big Data` folder in Spoon. If you need to configure any of the steps, you will find their documentation at `https:/ /help.pentaho.com/Documentation/8.1/Products/Data_Integration/ Transformation_Step_Reference`, or you can click on the **Help** button in their configuration windows. Also, there is the possibility to connect to the graph database Neo4J, through the installation of a dedicated plugin available via the Marketplace.

The **Marketplace** is a place to browse and install PDI plugins for different purposes, ranging from connecting to a source not available out of the box to implementing machine learning capabilities. The Marketplace is available via **Tools | Marketplace** in Spoon's main menu.

Getting data from other sources

So far, we have been getting data from plain files and databases. These are two of the most common data sources, but there are many more kinds of sources available in PDI, mainly grouped in, but not limited to, the `Input` folder. The following subsections will present some of the sources that we didn't cover in the previous sections, which are also of use.

XML and JSON

With PDI, you can read XML files or parse fields whose contents are in an XML structure. In both cases, you parse the XML with the **Get data from XML** input step. For specifying the fields to read, you use **XPath notation**. When the XML is very big or complex, there is an alternative step: **XML Input Stream (StAX)**.

Similarly, you can parse JSON structures with the **JSON Input** step. For specifying the fields in this case, you use **JSONPath notation**.

Also, you can parse both XML and JSON structures with JavaScript or Java code, by using the **Modified Java Script Value** step or the **User Defined Java Class** step, respectively.

System information and Kettle variables

There is also the possibility to obtain system information (for example, the current date or the JVM free memory). You can pick any of these and add them as a part of your flow. You can do so by using the **Get System Info** step. Take a look at the following screenshot:

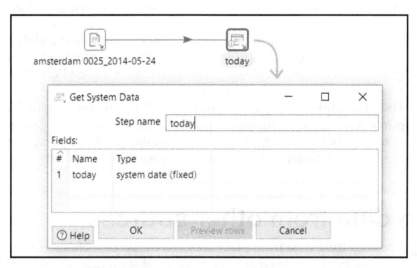

Getting system information

In this case, besides all of the fields coming from the input file, you will see a new field, named today, containing the system date. If you run a preview of the preceding step, you will see something like the following:

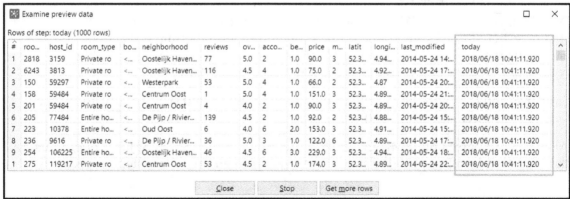

Previewing data with system information

As you can see, the value is repeated in all rows. You don't have to use this step in the middle of a stream. You can also create a dataset from scratch, as you did in the very first transformation created in Chapter 1, *Getting Started with PDI*.

Now, let's look at what we can do with variables. In the same way that you add system information, you can add the value of one or more Kettle variables, both user defined and predefined (for example, the name of the operating system, ${os.name}, or the home directory for the logged user, ${user.dir}). Just as in the previous example, after you get a variable, its value becomes a new field in the dataset. You can also create a whole new dataset, made up of Kettle variables, as follows:

1. Create a new transformation.
2. From the Job folder, drag a **Get Variables** step.
3. Double-click on the step and fill in the grid, as shown in the following screenshot:

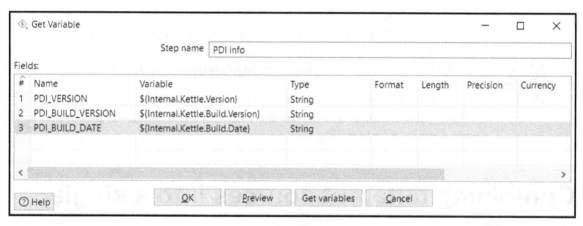

Getting variables

4. Close the window and run a preview. The result will be a dataset with three fields and a single row, shown as follows:

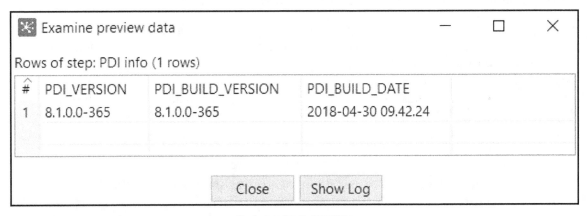

Previewing a dataset with variables

PDI can also pull streaming data. It supports **Java Messaging Service (JMS)**, MQTT protocol, and Apache Kafka. If you want to try any of these, you will find the corresponding consumer steps under the **Streaming** category.
As we mentioned previously, you can hit the **Help** button in the configuration window to find out the details for using each of the steps mentioned in the preceding section.

Combining different sources into a single dataset

In this chapter, you have been getting data from different kinds of sources. In all cases, the source of the data was unique; for example, a plain file or the result of a single query. However, what if we had more than one source, and we wanted to combine them and use them as a single dataset? In this section, you will learn how to deal with this very common situation.

Manipulating the metadata

Let's look at the first exercise again, where we read a file containing surveys. On that occasion, we read all of the information in the file. Now, suppose that we are interested in just a few fields: `room_id`, `room_type`, `neighborhood`, `overall_satisfaction`, `accommodates`, and `price`. Also, we want to rename some fields, and we want them in a different order.

There is a very easy way to do this, as follows:

1. Open the transformation created in the first exercise and save it under a different name. You can do so from **Main Menu** or **Main Toolbar**.
2. From the `Transform` folder, drag and drop a **Select values** step. Create a link from the **Text file input** file step to this new step.
3. Double-click on the **Select values** step. We will use it to select, order, and rename the fields. To do so, fill in the grid as follows:

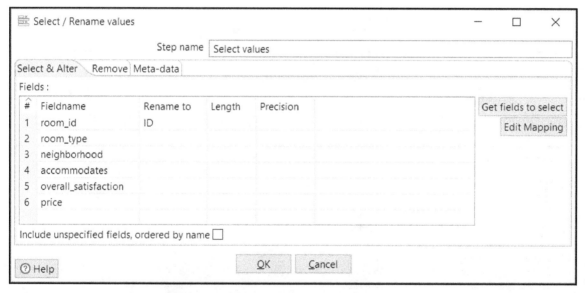

Configuring a Select values step

 You can save time by clicking on the **Get fields to select** button, which fills in the grid with all of the incoming fields. Then, you can adjust the values manually.

4. Close the window, and, with the mouse cursor over the icon, press *Ctrl +
   Spacebar*. A window will appear with the metadata coming from the step:

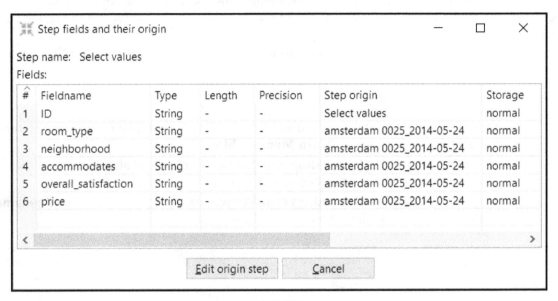

Output metadata

5. Close the window.
6. Keeping the step selected, run a preview. You will see the following:

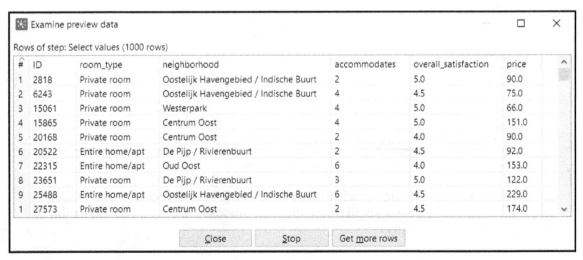

Previewing some data

The **Select values** step is normally used for selecting, reordering, and renaming fields, just like you did. It can also be used to change the metadata (the type or mask) of one or more fields.

 Note that in the **Text file input** step, you can name the fields differently, without the need to use a **Select values** step. However, you cannot alter the order of the incoming fields, nor can you ignore fields in the middle of the file. Therefore, you will need to use the **Select values** step later on.

Combining two different datasets into a single dataset

Continuing with the same exercise, suppose that we also want to read one of the files with a survey taken in 2017, and create a single dataset with information from both files. If you inspect the files, however, you will notice that the newest files don't have the same format as those with surveys taken in 2015. The fields are in a different order, and also there are new fields. If we intend to read both an old and a new file, we cannot do so using a single step. Let's work on the solution to this, as follows:

1. Open the transformation created previously.
2. Add a new **Text file input** step and configure it to read the `tomslee_airbnb_amsterdam_1476_2017-07-22.csv` file.
3. Run a preview, in order to check that the step is well configured.

4. Add a **Select values** step and configure it just as you did previously, in order to keep the same fields, in the same order, with the same names. The file that we are reading has a new field that also interests us: the name of the place. So, add this field, too. The configuration is shown in the following screenshot:

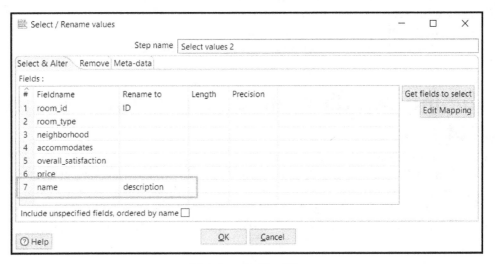

Select values configuration window

5. Make sure that the **Select values** step is selected, and run a preview. You will see something like the following:

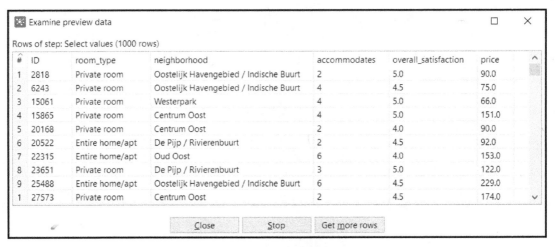

Previewing some data

6. Now, from the **Flow** folder, drag and drop a **Dummy (do nothing)** step, and create a link from the first **Select Values** step to that one. When asked for the kind of link, select **Main output of step**. The following shows what you have so far:

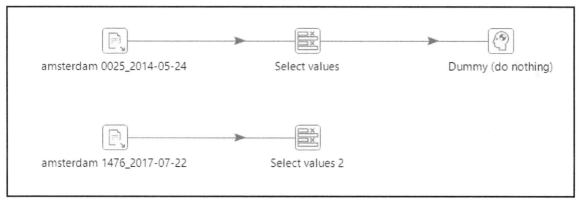

Designing a transformation

7. Now, in order to unify the datasets, create a hop from the second **Select values** step to the **Dummy** step. After selecting the kind of hop, a warning window will show up, telling you that the target step is receiving rows with mixed layouts.

The problem here is that you cannot combine datasets with different metadata. In this case, in the second stream of data, we have the `description` field not found in the other stream. We don't want to remove the field, so the solution is to add a field with the same name in the first dataset:

1. From the **Transform** folder, drag an **Add constants** step.
2. Drop the step over the link between the first **Select values** and the **Dummy** step.

3. You will be asked about splitting the hop. Click on **Yes**:

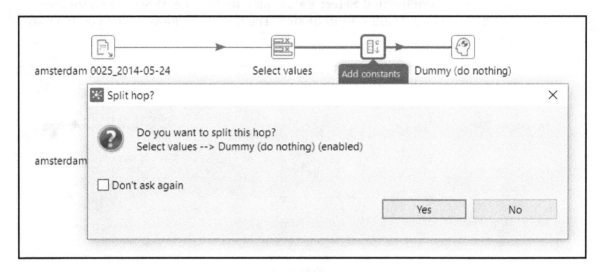

Splitting a hop

4. Double-click on the **Add constants** step and configure it to add the `description` field, with a default value:

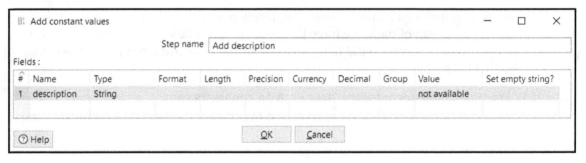

Configuring an Add constants step

5. Close the window.

6. Select the **Dummy** step and run a preview. You will see data coming from both streams of data:

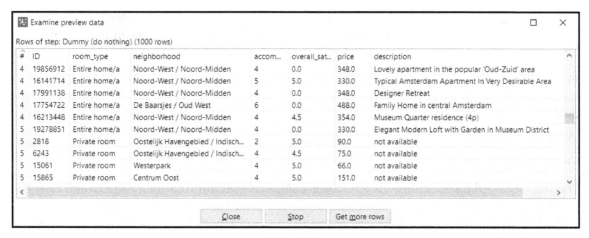

Previewing data

Whenever you want to combine two or more streams of data, you can proceed as you did here, making the necessary changes by adding or modifying fields, so that the output metadata of all of the streams is the same.

In this case, we used a **Dummy** step, which is mainly used as a placeholder for testing purposes; however, we could have used any other step instead.

Summary

In this chapter, you learned how to get data from different sources, converting it to PDI datasets.

First, you learned how to get data from plain files stored in your local system. You also had the opportunity to configure PDI to access compressed files and files stored in a Google Drive.

Having worked with files, you started to interact with relational databases. You learned how to configure a connection to a database, how to explore its content, and how to get data from it.

Finally, you were presented with sources other than plain files and databases, including XML and JSON sources and sources of system-related information.

Having explored the different options for getting external information, you learned how to combine two or more datasets into a single one. This task will be used not only for extracting and combining external sources but in many situations in your daily PDI work.

Now that you have the data, you are ready to transform it. You will learn how to do so in the next chapter.

Transforming Data

4

Transforming data is about manipulating the data that flows from step to step in a PDI transformation. There are many ways in which this transformation can be done. We can modify incoming data, change its datatype, add new fields, fix erroneous data, sort, group, and filter unwanted information, aggregate data in several ways, and more. In this chapter we will explain some of the possibilities.

The following is the list of topics that we will cover:

- Transforming data in different ways
- Sorting and aggregating data
- Filtering rows
- Looking up for data

Transforming data in different ways

So far, we have seen how to create a PDI dataset mainly using data coming from files or databases. Once you have the data, there are many things you can do with it depending on your particular needs. One very common requirement is to create new fields where the values are based on the values of existent fields.

The set of operations covered in this section is not a full list of the available options, but includes the most common ones, and will inspire you when you come to implement others.

The files that we will use in this section were built with data downloaded from www.numbeo.com, a site containing information about living conditions in cities and countries worldwide.

For learning the topics in this chapter, you are free to create your own data. However, if you want to reproduce the exercises exactly as they are explained, you will need the afore mentioned files from www.numbeo.com.

Before continuing, make sure you download the set of data that comes with the code bundle for the book.

Extracting data from existing fields

First, we will learn how to extract data from fields that exist in our dataset in order to generate new fields. For the first exercise, we will read a file containing data about the cost of living in Europe. The content of the file looks like this:

```
Rank City Cost of Living Index Rent Index Cost of Living Plus Rent Index
Groceries Index Restaurant Price Index Local Purchasing Power Index
1 Zurich, Switzerland 141.25 66.14 105.03 149.86 135.76 142.70
2 Geneva, Switzerland 134.83 71.70 104.38 138.98 129.74 130.96
3 Basel, Switzerland 130.68 49.68 91.61 127.54 127.22 139.01
4 Bern, Switzerland 128.03 43.57 87.30 132.70 119.48 112.71
5 Lausanne, Switzerland 127.50 52.32 91.24 126.59 132.12 127.95
6 Reykjavik, Iceland 123.78 57.25 91.70 118.15 133.19 88.95
...
```

As you can see, the city field also contains the country name. The purpose of this exercise is to extract the country name from this field. In order to do this, we will go through the following steps:

1. Create a new transformation and use a **Text file input** step to read the cost_of_living_europe.txt file.
2. Drag a **Split Fields** step from the **Transform** category and create a hop from the **Text file input** towards the **Split Fields** step.

3. Double-click the step and configure it, as shown in the following screenshot:

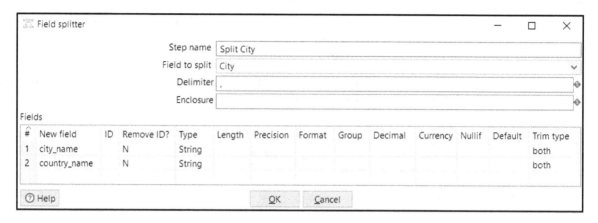

Configuring a Split Fields step

4. Close the window and run a preview. You will see the following:

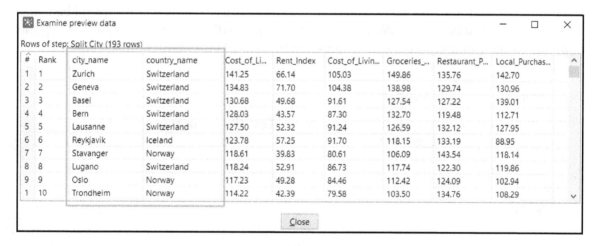

Previewing a transformation

As you can see, the **Split Fields** step can be used to split the value of a field into two or more new fields. This step is perfect for the purpose of obtaining the country name because the values were easy to parse. We had a value, then a comma, then another value. This is not always the case, but PDI has other steps for doing similar tasks. Let's look at another method for extracting pieces from a field.

This time, we will read a file containing common daily food items and their prices. The file has two fields—food and price—and looks as follows:

```
Food Price
Milk (regular), (0.25 liter) 0.19 €
Loaf of Fresh White Bread (125.00 g) 0.24 €
Rice (white), (0.10 kg) 0.09 €
Eggs (regular) (2.40) 0.33 €
Local Cheese (0.10 kg) 0.89 €
Chicken Breasts (Boneless, Skinless), (0.15 kg) 0.86 €
...
```

Suppose that we want to split the `Food` field into three fields for the name, quantity, and number of units respectively. Taking the value in the first row, `Milk (regular), (0.25 liter)`, as an example, the name would be `Milk (regular)`, the quantity would be `0.25`, and the unit would be `liter`. We cannot solve this as we did before, but we can use regular expressions instead. In this case, the expression to use will be `(.+)\(([0-9.]+)( liter| g| kg| head|)\).*`.

Let's try it using the following steps:

1. Create a new transformation and use a **Text file input** step to read the `recommended_food.txt` file.

> In order to define the `Price` as a number, use the format `#.00 €`.

2. Drag a **Regex Evaluation** step from the **Scripting** category and create a hop from the **Text file input** toward this new step.

3. Double-click the step and configure it as shown in the following screenshot. Don't forget to check the **Create fields for capture groups** option:

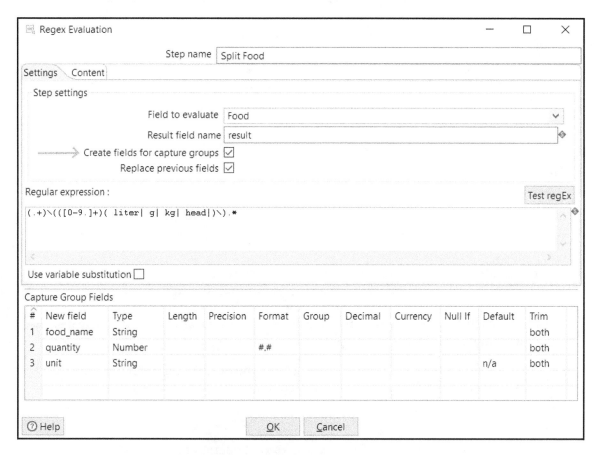

Configuring a Regex Evaluation step

4. Close the window and run a preview. You will see the following:

Previewing a transformation

The **RegEx Evaluation** step can be used just to evaluate whether or not a field matches a regular expression, or to generate new fields, as in this case. By capturing groups, we were able to create a new field for each group captured from the original field. You will also notice a field named `result`, which in our example has a `Y` as its value. This `Y` means that the original field matched the given expression.

Note that while the **Split Fields** step removes the original field from the dataset, the **RegEx Evaluation** step does not.

These are not the only steps that will allow this kind of operation.

Feel free to browse the list of steps—mainly those in the **Transformation** folder—and try your own solutions.

More ways to create new fields

Besides just extracting data from the incoming fields, we can also combine the fields by performing arithmetic operations between them, concatenating String fields, and using other methods. Just as we did in the previous section, let's expand on a simple example that will serve you as a model for creating your own process.

For this tutorial, we will continue to use the file containing data about the cost of living. This time, we want to generate a new field that creates a new index out of the average of the restaurant price index and the groceries index. To do this, we will go through the following steps:

1. Create a new transformation and use a **Text file input** step to read the `cost_of_living_europe.txt` file.

> Alternatively, you can open the transformation we created previously and save it under a new name.

2. Drag a **Calculator** step from the **Transform** category and create a hop from the **Text file input** toward the calculator.
3. Double-click the step and configure it as shown in the following screenshot:

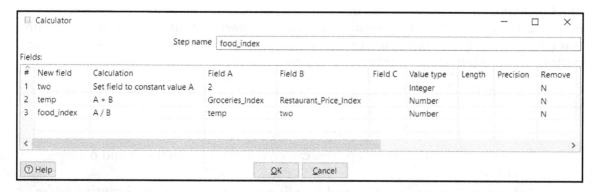

#	New field	Calculation	Field A	Field B	Field C	Value type	Length	Precision	Remove
1	two	Set field to constant value A	2			Integer			N
2	temp	A + B	Groceries_Index	Restaurant_Price_Index		Number			N
3	food_index	A / B	temp	two		Number			N

Step name: food_index

Configuring a Calculator step

4. Close the window and run a preview. You will see the following:

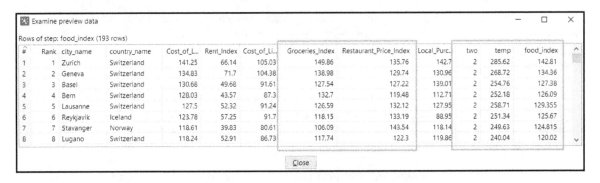

#	Rank	city_name	country_name	Cost_of_L...	Rent_Index	Cost_of_Li...	Groceries_Index	Restaurant_Price_Index	Local_Purc..	two	temp	food_index
1	1	Zurich	Switzerland	141.25	66.14	105.03	149.86	135.76	142.7	2	285.62	142.81
2	2	Geneva	Switzerland	134.83	71.7	104.38	138.98	129.74	130.96	2	268.72	134.36
3	3	Basel	Switzerland	130.68	49.68	91.61	127.54	127.22	139.01	2	254.76	127.38
4	4	Bern	Switzerland	128.03	43.57	87.3	132.7	119.48	112.71	2	252.18	126.09
5	5	Lausanne	Switzerland	127.5	52.32	91.24	126.59	132.12	127.95	2	258.71	129.355
6	6	Reykjavik	Iceland	123.78	57.25	91.7	118.15	133.19	88.95	2	251.34	125.67
7	7	Stavanger	Norway	118.61	39.83	80.61	106.09	143.54	118.14	2	249.63	124.815
8	8	Lugano	Switzerland	118.24	52.91	86.73	117.74	122.3	119.86	2	240.04	120.02

Previewing a transformation

As you can deduce from the configuration window, with the **Calculator** step, we can create new fields by using temporary fields in the way. In the final dataset, we can see each temporary field—two and temp, in our example—as a new column.

> If you don't need those temporary fields in the final dataset, look for the **Remove** column in the configuration window and change its value to Y.

The **Calculator** step is a handy step that can be used for performing many common types of operations, such as arithmetic operations (adding, subtracting, and so on), operations with text (concatenating, converting to uppercase, and so on), operations with dates (extracting parts of a date, subtracting dates, and so on), among others.

Of course, there is a simpler way for doing the calculation in the last transformation. Let's try it:

1. Save the previous transformation under a different name.
2. Remove the **Calculator** step. You can do this just by selecting it and pressing *Delete*.
3. Drag and drop a **User Defined Java Expression** step from the **Scripting** folder. Create a hop from the **Text file input** step toward this new step.
4. Double-click the step and configure it as shown in the following screenshot:

Configuring a Java Expression step

5. Close the window and run a preview. You should see exactly the same result as before.

The **Java Expression** step is a powerful step that allows you to create fields of any type—not just numbers—by using a wide variety of expressions, as long as they can be expressed in a single line using Java syntax. In the last example, using the **Java Expression** step was simpler than doing the same with a **Calculator** step. Depending on the case, it can be more convenient to use one or the other.

This was just an example that showed you how to add new fields based on the fields in your dataset. There are many steps available, and with different purposes. You will find them mainly in the **Transform** folder, but there are some others in different folders in the **Design** tab. No matter which step you pick, the way you use it is always the same. You add the step at the end of the stream and then configure it properly according to your needs.

Sorting and aggregating data

In the previous section, we learned how to work with individual fields—for example, by creating new ones or modifying existent ones. The operations were applied row by row. In this section, we will not look at individual rows, but we will instead learn to observe and work on the dataset as a unit.

Sorting data

Sorting the dataset is a very useful and common task. Sorting is really easy to do in PDI, and we will demonstrate it with a simple transformation. We will take the files of the surveys that we used in the previous chapter, and we will sort the data by `neighborhood` and `room_type` columns, and then by the `reviews` column in descending order. In order to do this, go through the following steps:

1. Open any of the transformations created in the last chapter that read files with surveys. Save the transformation with a different name.
2. Drag a **Sort rows** step from the **Transform** folder and create a hop from the **Text file input** toward this new step.
3. Double-click the step and configure it as shown in the following screenshot:

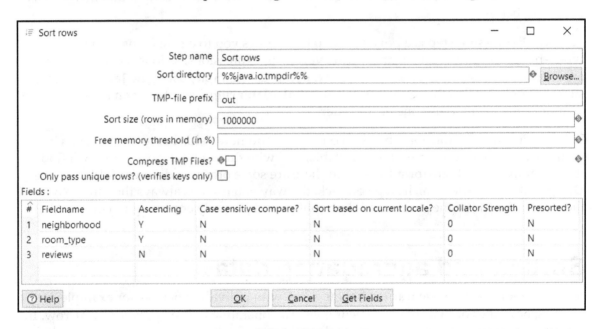

Configuring a Sort rows step

4. Close the window.

5. After the **Sort rows** step, add a **Select values** step. So far, you will have a series of steps resembling the one shown in the following screenshot:

Designing a Transformation

6. Configure the **Select values** step as shown in the following screenshot:

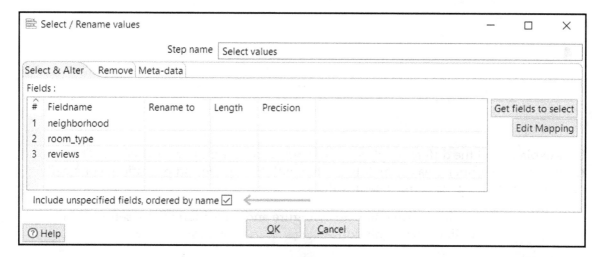

Configuring a Select values step

 Adding the **Select values** step is not mandatory, but it will make it easy to see how the data was sorted. Note that we didn't select a subset of fields; we just reordered them.

7. Close the window. With the **Select values** step selected, run a preview. You will see the data sorted as expected, as shown in the following image:

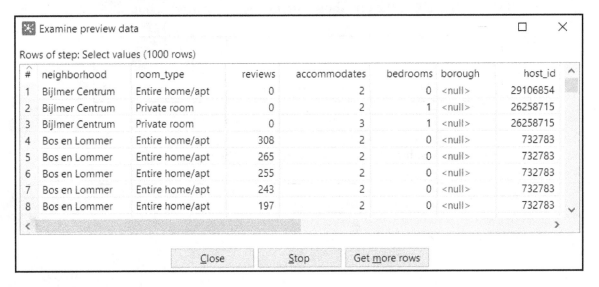

Examine preview data

Rows of step: Select values (1000 rows)

#	neighborhood	room_type	reviews	accommodates	bedrooms	borough	host_id
1	Bijlmer Centrum	Entire home/apt	0	2	0	<null>	29106854
2	Bijlmer Centrum	Private room	0	2	1	<null>	26258715
3	Bijlmer Centrum	Private room	0	3	1	<null>	26258715
4	Bos en Lommer	Entire home/apt	308	2	0	<null>	732783
5	Bos en Lommer	Entire home/apt	265	2	0	<null>	732783
6	Bos en Lommer	Entire home/apt	255	2	0	<null>	732783
7	Bos en Lommer	Entire home/apt	243	2	0	<null>	732783
8	Bos en Lommer	Entire home/apt	197	2	0	<null>	732783

Close   Stop   Get more rows

Previewing sorted data

Let's explain a bit the different options in the **Sort rows** configuration window. The textboxes in the upper area are mainly related with tuning the sort operation. For small datasets you can just leave the default values.

For understanding how to configure and understand these settings check the online documentation at `https://wiki.pentaho.com/display/EAI/Sort+rows`

Now let's talk about the grid. The different columns in the grid of the configuration window give PDI indications for sorting. For example you could tell PDI to order a column in ascendent way (**Ascending** = Y) or to perform locale-sensitive String comparison (**Sort based on current locale?** = Y). All the columns have default values, so you only have to specify the fieldnames, unless you want a behavior different from the default.

Sorting the data can be a task in and of itself, but it is also used for advanced operations, as we will soon learn. One particular use of the **Sort rows** step is for creating unique lists. For instance, suppose that you want to build a list of the neighborhoods where the surveys took place. If you sort the previous dataset just by neighborhood, you will have all the values, but they will be repeated. If you check the **Only pass unique rows? (verifies keys only)** option, PDI will remove the duplicates.

Note that the uniqueness is verified only on the list of fields by which you are sorting—neighborhood, in this case.

Take into account that the **Sort rows** will only remove rows, not columns. If you preview the dataset after this sort operation, you will see the following:

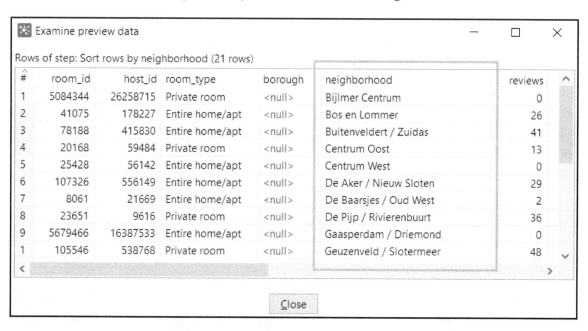

#	room_id	host_id	room_type	borough	neighborhood	reviews
1	5084344	26258715	Private room	\<null\>	Bijlmer Centrum	0
2	41075	178227	Entire home/apt	\<null\>	Bos en Lommer	26
3	78188	415830	Entire home/apt	\<null\>	Buitenveldert / Zuidas	41
4	20168	59484	Private room	\<null\>	Centrum Oost	13
5	25428	56142	Entire home/apt	\<null\>	Centrum West	0
6	107326	556149	Entire home/apt	\<null\>	De Aker / Nieuw Sloten	29
7	8061	21669	Entire home/apt	\<null\>	De Baarsjes / Oud West	2
8	23651	9616	Private room	\<null\>	De Pijp / Rivierenbuurt	36
9	5679466	16387533	Entire home/apt	\<null\>	Gaasperdam / Driemond	0
1	105546	538768	Private room	\<null\>	Geuzenveld / Slotermeer	48

Rows of step: Sort rows by neighborhood (21 rows)

Previewing data sorted with the unique row option

In order to complete the exercise and just keep the neighborhood field, you may use a **Select values** step.

Aggregating data

To aggregate data, we perform an operation on a group of rows, such as counting the number of rows or calculating the average value of a particular column. In PDI, there is a commonly used step for performing this kind of operation: the **Group by** step.
In this section, we will learn to use that **Group by** step. We will take the dataset of the cost of living, and we will calculate the average cost-of-living index by country. To do this, we will go through the following steps:

1. Open the first version of the transformation that reads the cost of living file—the one that split the city and country name—and save it under a different name.
2. After the last step, add a **Sort rows** step. Use it to sort the rows by `country_name`.
3. After the **Sort rows** step, add a **Group by** step. You will find it under the **Statistics** folder.
4. Double-click the step and configure it as shown in the following screenshot:

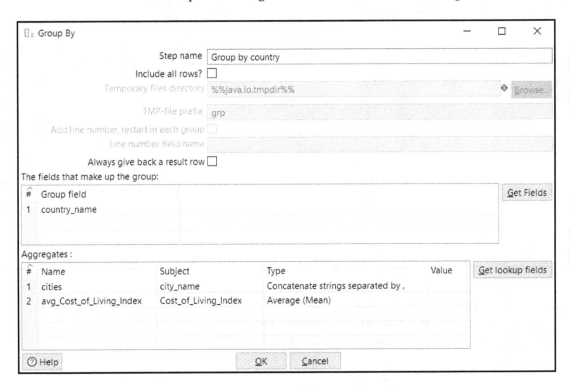

Configuring a Group by step

5. Close the window. You will be warned about the order of rows. Click on **Close**.

6. Select both the **Sort rows** and the **Group by** steps. To do this, click the first step, and then press and hold *Ctrl* and click on the second.

7. Press *F10* to run a preview, and then click on **Quick Launch**. A small window will show up with the name of the steps selected.

8. Click on the **Sort rows** option and then click on **Show**. The preview window will appear:

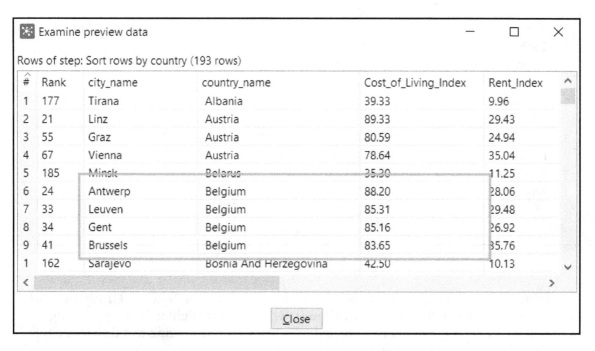

Previewing sorted data

9. Without closing that window, click on the other option in the menu—the **Group by** option—and click on **Show**. A new preview window will appear:

#	country_name	cities	avg_Cost_of_Living_Index
⊞ Examine preview data		— ☐ ✕	
Rows of step: Group by country (40 rows)			
1	Albania	Tirana	39.33
2	Austria	Linz, Graz, Vienna	82.8533333333
3	Belarus	Minsk	35.3
4	Belgium	Antwerp, Leuven, Gent, Brussels	85.58
5	Bosnia And Herzegovina	Sarajevo, Banja Luka	41.175
6	Bulgaria	Sofia, Varna, Burgas, Plovdiv	41.6175
7	Croatia	Split, Rijeka, Zagreb, Osijek	56.1575
8	Czech Republic	Prague, Brno, Olomouc, Ostrava	48.725
9	Denmark	Copenhagen, Arhus, Aalborg	93.5633333333
1	Estonia	Tallinn, Tartu	58.0
1	Finland	Helsinki, Tampere, Turku	85.7166666667

Close

Previewing aggregated data

By having both preview windows open, it's easier to understand how the **Group by** works. As an example, look at the values for Belgium, which are highlighted in the preceding screenshots. In the original dataset, we had four rows, each belonging to a different city. After the **Group by** step, we see two new fields: the list of cities belonging to that group—Antwerp, Leuven, Gent, Brussels—and the average index—85.58—which is exactly the average of the index for those four cities: (88.20 + 85.31 + 85.16 + 83.65) / 4.

Note that the step operates on consecutive rows. As the original set was not ordered by country, if you didn't sort, then the result would have been different.

To summarize, the **Group by** step performs aggregations on groups of rows. The fields that make up the groups are defined in the upper grid of the configuration window (in our example, we only grouped by the `country_name` field). In the lower grid, there is one row for each new field. In the example, we performed two different kinds of aggregation: we concatenated string values and we also calculated the average of a numeric value.

 If you take a look at the drop-down list of options under the **Type** column in the **Group by** step, you will see a lot of possible operations, including `sum`, `count`, `first value`, and more.

Note that after the aggregation, the dataset is no longer the same: We have a new dataset built by the group columns—the fields in the upper grid—and the aggregate columns—the fields in the lower grid.

As a final comment on this step, let's say that it's not necessary to group the rows by a list of fields. You may want to run an aggregation over the whole set of rows. Suppose that you have the file containing the common food items and want to know how much you should invest in food in total. This number is just the sum of the price field, calculated for all the rows in the dataset. Let's quickly see how you would compute this:

1. Open the transformation that read the food file, and save it with a different name.

2. After the last step, add a **Group by** step. Double-click the step and configure it as shown in the following screenshot:

Configuring a Group by step

3. Close the window. With the step selected, run a preview. You will then see the following:

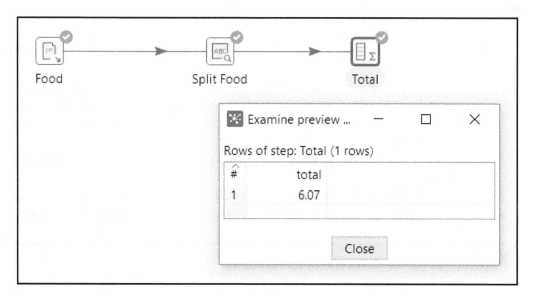

Previewing a transformation

Filtering rows

Until now, we have been enriching our dataset with new data. Now we will do the exact opposite: we will discard unwanted information. We already know how to keep a subset of fields and discard the rest: We do it by using the **Select values** step. Now it's time to keep only the rows that we are interested on.

Filtering rows upon conditions

To demonstrate how to filter rows with PDI, we will work again with the survey files. This time, we will read a set of files, and will keep only the locations with more than three rooms. The main step we will be using is the **Filter rows** step. Go through the following steps:

1. Create a transformation and use a **Text file input** step to read the files containing the surveys carried in 2015.

You are free to read a different set of files, but if you read this set, you will be able to compare your results with the results shown in the following screenshots.

2. After the **Text file input** step, add a **Filter rows** step. You will find it in the **Flow** folder.

3. In the main area of the configuration window, there is a place for building the condition for filtering. You construct the condition by selecting different fields and operators from a series of drop-down lists. The condition that we want to apply to our rows is bedrooms > 3.

4. Click on the first **<field>** option. A list will appear with the full list of fields. Select **bedroom**.

5. To the right, there is the operator list. Pick the **>** (greater than) option.

6. Click on **<value>** and type 3. The configuration window should look like this:

Configuring a Filter rows step

7. Click on **OK** to close the window.

8. After the **Filter rows** step, add a **Dummy** step. Remember that you can find it in the **Flow** folder. When asked for the kind of hop, select **Main output of step**.

9. With the **Dummy** step selected, run a preview. You will only see rows belonging to places with more than three bedrooms:

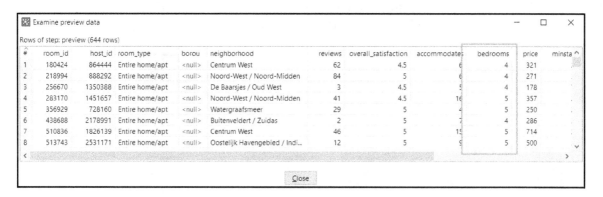

Previewing filtered rows

10. Now save and run the transformation.

11. Look at the **Step Metrics** in the **Execution Results** window. You will see that 25350 rows come into the **Filter rows** step, but only 1961—the number under the **Written** column—pass the filter.

Now suppose that we want to slightly modify the condition so that we will keep only places with more than three rooms or that can accommodate at least five people. This new condition can be expressed as `bedrooms > 3 OR accommodates > 4`. We already have the first part of our condition. Let's add the second part by going through the following steps:

1. Double-click the **Filter rows** step, and click on the plus sign in the upper-right corner of the condition area. A new empty subcondition will appear:

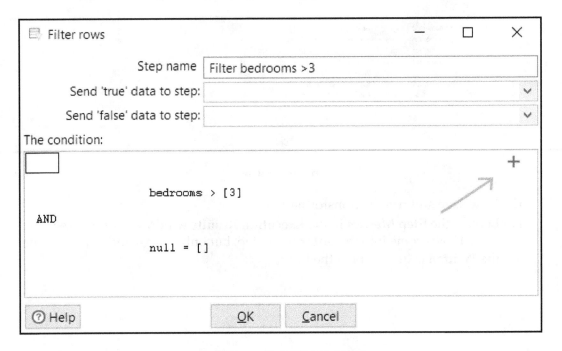

Building a condition in a Filter rows step

2. Click on the **AND** operator and change it to **OR**.
3. Click on **null = []**. You will be prompted to enter the second part of the condition. Enter the `accommodates > 4` condition by using the drop-down lists, just as you did before.

4. Click on **OK**. You will then see the following:

Configuring a Filter rows step

5. Close the window.
6. Select the **Dummy** step and run a preview. You will see the new filter applied, showing only rows with `bedroom>3` or `accomodates>4`.

Now, suppose that you want a more complex condition: places with more than three bedrooms, or that accommodate more than four people, and with a price below 200. It is possible to create this condition with the **Filter rows** step, but as the conditions get more complicated, it's also more complicated to configure the step. Fortunately, there is another step that allows us to do this in a simpler fashion: the **Java Filter** step. To put it in place, go through the following steps:

1. Create a new transformation.
2. Use a **Text file input** step for reading the survey files. This time, in the **Fields** tab set a default value for the `bedrooms` and `accommodates` fields—for instance, it could be 0 or -1.
3. After the **Text file input** step, add a **Java Filter** step. You will find it inside the **Flow** folder.

4. Double-click the step. In the **Condition (Java expression)** textbox, type `(bedrooms>3 || accommodates >4) && price<200`.

5. Click on **OK**, and run a preview. You will only see the rows that match the preceding condition.

Note that configuring this step was much simpler than configuring a **Filter rows** step. Depending on the characteristics of your condition, you will prefer one over the other.

 Null values in the fields used in a **Java expression** would cause a failure of the transformation. That was the reason for setting the default values while reading the files.

Splitting the stream upon conditions

In the previous examples, we applied a filter and discarded the rows that didn't match a given condition. It may be the case that you don't want to discard any row. You might simply want to apply different treatments to the rows that match and those that don't match a particular condition. This can be accomplished in a simple way. Suppose that you want to separate the locations with private rooms from the rest of the locations:

1. Create a transformation and read the files containing the surveys.
2. After the input step, add a **Filter rows** step.
3. Double-click the step and use it to create the `Room_type = Private room` filter.
4. Drag two **Dummy** steps from the **Flow** folder to the work area.

 We are using the **Dummy** steps as placeholders for testing purposes. You can use any step instead if you prefer.

5. Create a hop from the **Filter rows** step toward one of the **Dummy** steps. When asked for the kind of hop, select **Result is TRUE**.

6. Now create a hop from the **Filter rows** step toward the other **Dummy** step. This time, select **Result is FALSE**. Feel free to rename the **Dummy** steps as well. At this point, you should have something similar to the steps shown in the following screenshot:

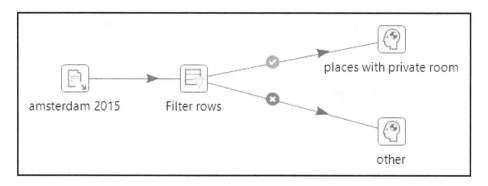

Transformation with a Filter rows step

7. Click on the first **Dummy** step and run a preview. You will only see the places with private rooms:

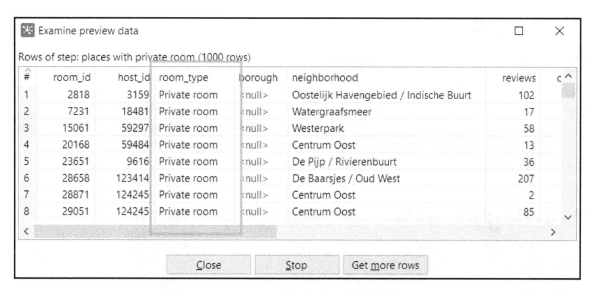

Previewing some data

8. Click on the second **Dummy** step and run a preview. You will only see the places with room types different from private rooms.

If you take a look at the **Step Metrics**, you will see that the **Filter rows** step passes all the rows—the number of rows entering the step is the same as the number of rows leaving the step. Also, looking at the **Read** column, you will see that the whole set is split in two: The rows that match the condition—4696—are read by one **Dummy** step while the rest of the rows are read by the other **Dummy** step, as shown in the following screenshot:

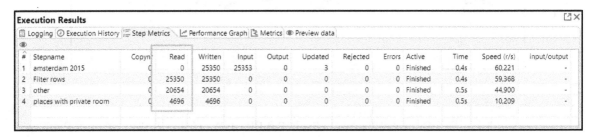

#	Stepname	Copyn	Read	Written	Input	Output	Updated	Rejected	Errors	Active	Time	Speed (r/s)	input/output
1	amsterdam 2015	0	0	25350	25353	0	3	0	0	Finished	0.4s	60,221	-
2	Filter rows	0	25350	25350	0	0	0	0	0	Finished	0.4s	59,368	-
3	other	0	20654	20654	0	0	0	0	0	Finished	0.5s	44,900	-
4	places with private room	0	4696	4696	0	0	0	0	0	Finished	0.5s	10,209	-

Step Metrics

Looking up for data

In all the transformations that we have created so far, we had single streams of data. We could, however, create more than one stream, with data coming from different sources. The streams can eventually be merged together—as was the case when we merged data coming from different files in the previous chapters—or they can also be used for looking up data, as we will learn in this section.

Looking for data in a secondary stream

Looking for data in a secondary stream is a common requirement when the data you need comes from a source that is different from your main data—for example, if your data comes from a database, and you need to look up related data in an XML file. In this section, you will learn how to implement this kind of lookup through a simple exercise: We will have a list of European cities, and we will look for their cost of living indexes that are located in a different source. To do this, go through the following steps:

For this exercise, we will use a file with a list of European cities and their populations. The data was obtained from `https://en.wikipedia.org/wiki/List_of_European_cities_by_population_within_city_limits`.

1. Create a new transformation and use a **Text file input** step for reading the `europe.txt` file.

2. Run a preview. You will see the following:

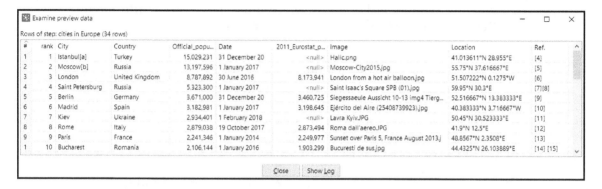

Previewing European cities' populations

Before looking up the cost-of-living index, let's do some cleaning. We will remove some references—in this case, [a] in `Istanbul[a]`. To do this, we will remove the characters that match the regular expression \[.+\].

3. Add a **Replace in string** step. You will find it in the **Transform** folder.

4. Double-click the step and configure it as shown in the following screenshot:

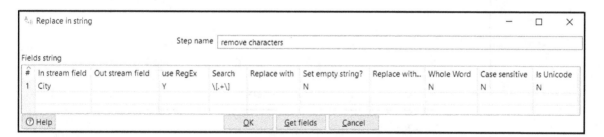

Configuring a Replace in string step

5. Close the step and run a preview. You will then see how the city names with references were cleaned up.

We fixed the values with a **Replace in string** step, but there are alternative ways for doing this. For instance, we could have used a **Split Fields**, a **Regex Evaluation**, or a **Java Expression** step instead.

6. After this step, add a **Select values** step and use it to keep only the `rank`, `City`, `Country`, and `Official_population` fields.

Now that we have the main data, we want to look for the cost-of-living index for each city. We have that information in another file that we already used in earlier examples. We will reuse part of this work. Let's go through the following steps:

1. Open one of the transformations that read the indexes file and that split the city and country name fields.
2. Select all the steps, copy them with *Ctrl + C*, and paste them with *Ctrl + V* into the transformation that we are developing. You should have the following by the end of this process:

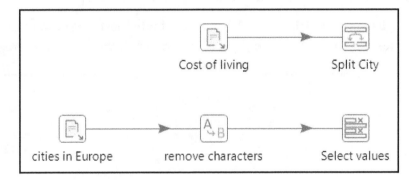

Designing a transformation

3. Drag a **Stream lookup** step from the **Transform** folder to the work area. Create a hop from the last step in each stream toward this new step. When asked for the kind of hop, select **Main output of step**.
4. Double-click the **Stream lookup** step. Configure it as shown in the following screenshot:

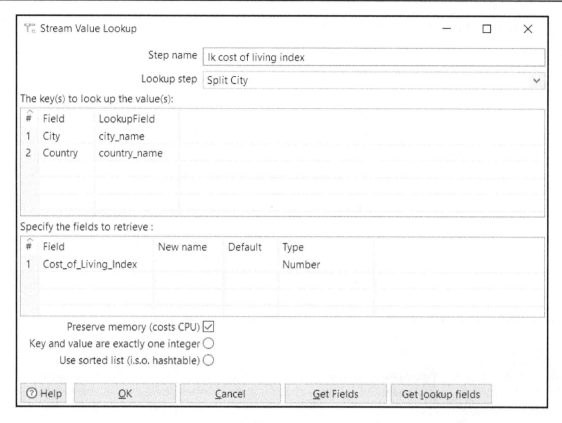

Configuring a Stream lookup step

5. Close the step. You will see how the hop coming from the lookup stream changed its look and feel. The transformation looks as shown in the following screenshot:

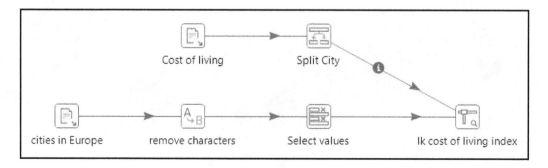

Transformation with a Stream lookup step

6. Select the Stream lookup step and run a preview:

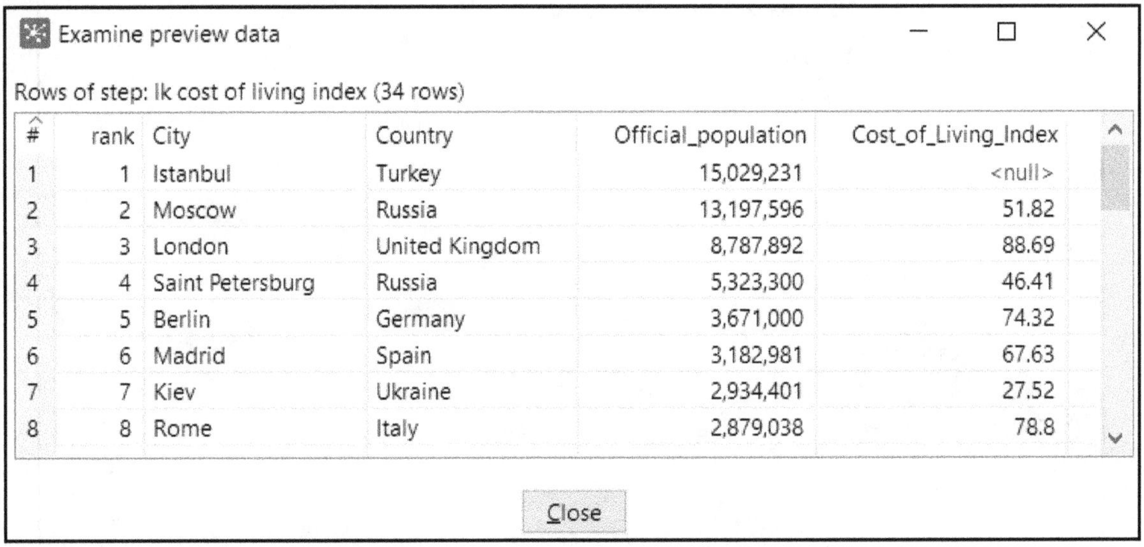

#	rank	City	Country	Official_population	Cost_of_Living_Index
1	1	Istanbul	Turkey	15,029,231	\<null\>
2	2	Moscow	Russia	13,197,596	51.82
3	3	London	United Kingdom	8,787,892	88.69
4	4	Saint Petersburg	Russia	5,323,300	46.41
5	5	Berlin	Germany	3,671,000	74.32
6	6	Madrid	Spain	3,182,981	67.63
7	7	Kiev	Ukraine	2,934,401	27.52
8	8	Rome	Italy	2,879,038	78.8

Examine preview data — Rows of step: lk cost of living index (34 rows) — Close

Previewing data

As you can observe in the preview window, a new field was added to the main stream: the `cost_of_living_index` field. For each city, the value was taken from the secondary stream—the one that has all the indexes for a list of cities in Europe. A way to confirm this is by inspecting the output metadata of the step. You do this by positioning the cursor over the **Stream lookup** step and pressing the *spacebar*. In the window that appears, the **Step origin** column will tell you where each field was created in your dataset, as shown in the following screenshot:

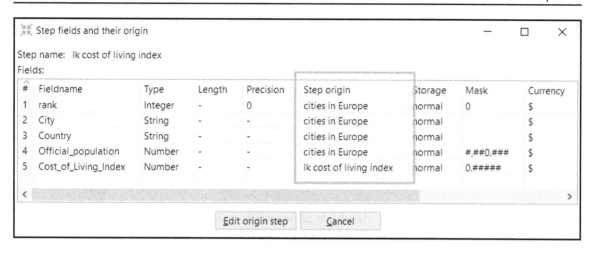

Output metadata

Let's briefly explain the way you configure the **Stream lookup** step and how it works:

1. The first thing you do is indicate which of the incoming streams will be looked into (**Lookup step**). In this case, we want to look for data in the stream containing the indexes.

2. Then you have to fill two grids. In the upper grid, you indicate the keys—that is, the fields that will be used for the looking up operation. In the example, the keys in the main stream were Country and City. The matching fields in the secondary stream were country_name and city_name.

3. In the lower grid, you specify the field or fields that you want to get from the secondary stream should the lookup succeed.

The **Stream lookup** step looks for exact matches. So, if you don't get the same results, a possible reason could be that the country or city fields have leading spaces. To remove them make sure that, in the **Split field** step, you set the **Trim type** column to **both**.

In our example, most of the cities in the main file were found in the stream that had indexes. In the cases where the lookup failed, the value for the index was set to null. You can set a default value instead by typing it in the lower grid of the configuration window.

Looking up data in a database

Looking up data that is stored in a database is a particular case of the process that we use for looking up data in general. We have one or more fields that are the keys for looking up data in a secondary source of data. However, when that secondary source is a database, the way we look through it is different.

 For the tutorial in this section, we will use the sports database that we used in the previous chapter.

To learn how to look up data in a database table, we will start with a file containing information about injured people. The file looks like the following code:

```
person_id;injury_type;injury_date
153;elbow;2007-07-09
186;fingers;2007-07-15
198;shoulder;2007-07-15
213;elbow;2007-07-16
378;elbow;2007-07-24
391;lower-back;2007-07-29
400;elbow;2007-07-21
407;lower-back;2007-07-15
...
```

We have the `person_id` fields and we want to get the names of the people that they correspond to, which can be found in the `display_names` table in the sports database. We can do this by going through the following steps:

1. Create a new transformation.
2. With a **Text file input** step, read the `injuries.txt` file.

   The `display_names` table contains more than just the names of people. It has a field named `entity_type` that has the value `persons`. So to look up the values, we will need a composed key made up of the `person_id` and the `entity_type` fields. In order to look up the proper value, we need that constant value in our main stream.

3. After the **Text file input** step, add an **Add constants** step. This step is located under the **Transform** folder.

4. Double-click the step and configure it as shown in the following screenshot:

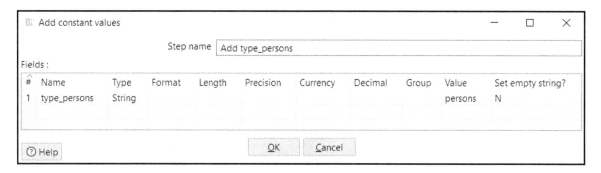

Configure an **Add constants** step.

5. Run a preview. You will see the following:

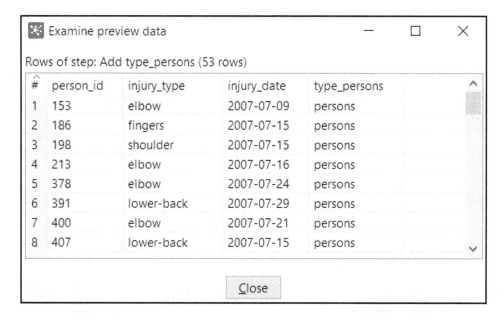

Previewing some data

6. From the **Lookup** folder, drag and drop a **Database lookup** step. Create a hop from the previous step toward this one.

7. Double-click the step and configure it as shown in the following screenshot:

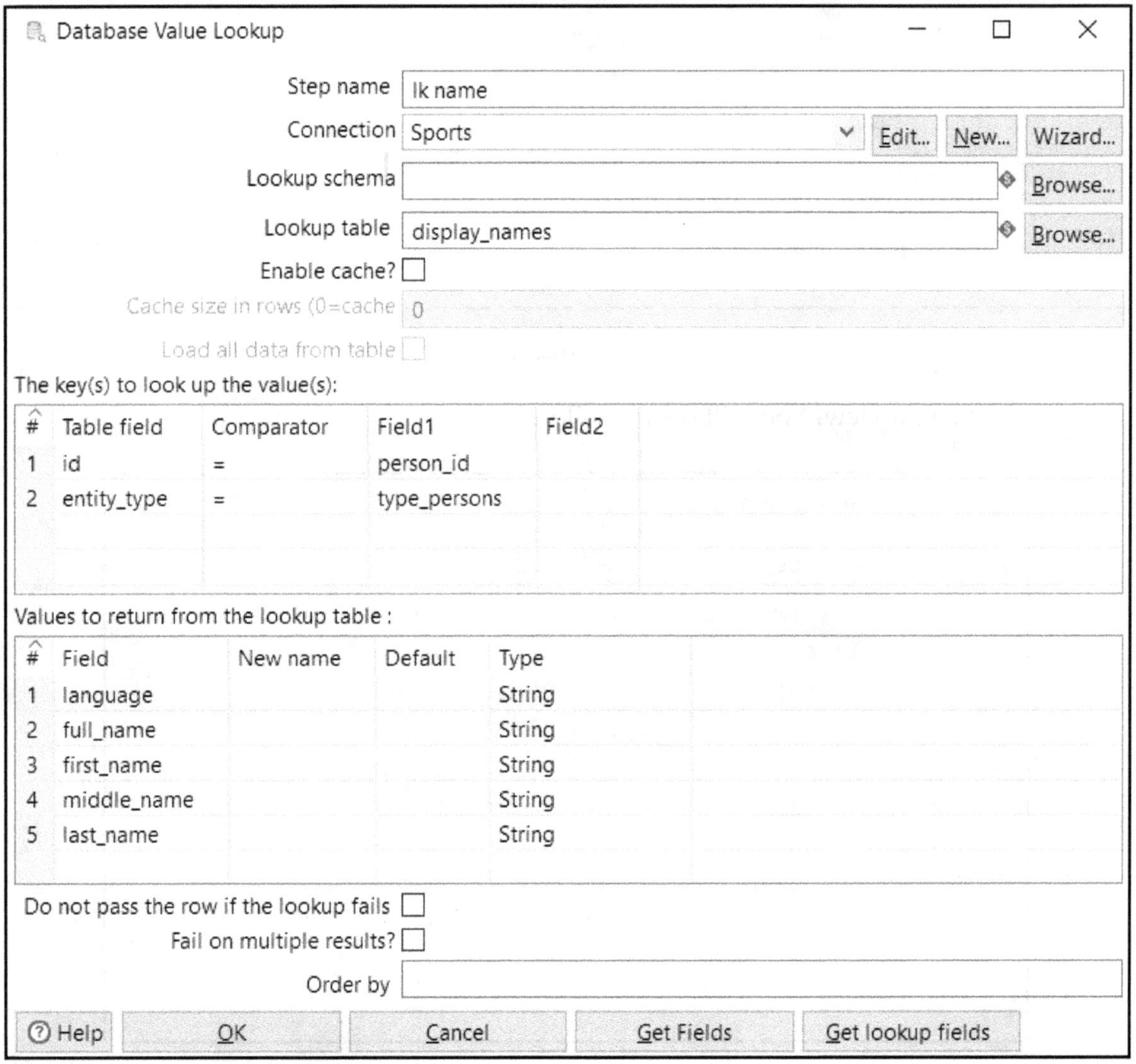

Database Value Lookup	— □ ✕

Step name	lk name
Connection	Sports ∨ Edit... New... Wizard...
Lookup schema	◈ Browse...
Lookup table	display_names ◈ Browse...
Enable cache?	☐
Cache size in rows (0=cache	0
Load all data from table	☐

The key(s) to look up the value(s):

#	Table field	Comparator	Field1	Field2
1	id	=	person_id	
2	entity_type	=	type_persons	

Values to return from the lookup table :

#	Field	New name	Default	Type
1	language			String
2	full_name			String
3	first_name			String
4	middle_name			String
5	last_name			String

Do not pass the row if the lookup fails	☐
Fail on multiple results?	☐
Order by	

⊙ Help	OK	Cancel	Get Fields	Get lookup fields

Configuring a Database lookup step

8. Run a preview. You will see the names of the people added to your stream, as shown in the following screenshot:

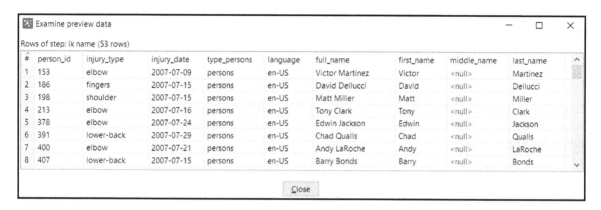

#	person_id	injury_type	injury_date	type_persons	language	full_name	first_name	middle_name	last_name
1	153	elbow	2007-07-09	persons	en-US	Victor Martinez	Victor	<null>	Martinez
2	186	fingers	2007-07-15	persons	en-US	David Dellucci	David	<null>	Dellucci
3	198	shoulder	2007-07-15	persons	en-US	Matt Miller	Matt	<null>	Miller
4	213	elbow	2007-07-16	persons	en-US	Tony Clark	Tony	<null>	Clark
5	378	elbow	2007-07-24	persons	en-US	Edwin Jackson	Edwin	<null>	Jackson
6	391	lower-back	2007-07-29	persons	en-US	Chad Qualls	Chad	<null>	Qualls
7	400	elbow	2007-07-21	persons	en-US	Andy LaRoche	Andy	<null>	LaRoche
8	407	lower-back	2007-07-15	persons	en-US	Barry Bonds	Barry	<null>	Bonds

Previewing data

As you can see, the configuration window in a **Database lookup** is quite similar to the configuration window in a **Stream lookup**. In the upper grid, you specify the conditions for looking up, and in the lower grid, you list the fields that you want to get from the table should the lookup succeed.

> The **Database lookup** step has several configuration settings. It's recommended that you hit the **Help** button in the configuration window of the step and take a look at the documentation. Doing that you will learn how to configure the step properly depending on the use case.

Summary

In this chapter, we transformed PDI datasets in several ways. First, we learned to transform data at row level by combining values, extracting pieces of a value, creating new fields, just to mention some of the different operations. For each particular operation, we learned how PDI offers different ways of doing the same thing. We encouraged you to experiment with different steps and adopt the ones that best fit your needs.

Then, we learned how to sort data and then aggregate it by adding values and calculating averages, among other common aggregate operations.

After having transformed the dataset, we learned how to filter unwanted data, either discarding it or redirecting it to alternative flows.

At the end of the chapter, we enriched the datasets by looking up external data—both in databases and in secondary streams—and adding it to our main flow.

Now that we have seen the main ways of transforming data coming in from different sources, we are ready to load that data into multiple destinations. This is the subject of the next chapter.

5
Loading Data

In this chapter, we will explain how to save transformation output in files and relational databases. In addition, we will cover how to load data into a datamart.

The following topics will be covered in this chapter:

- Generating different kinds of files
- Inserting and updating data into database tables
- Loading dimensions
- Loading fact tables

Generating different kinds of files

After loading and transforming your data in many ways, you will want to send the results to a destination. In particular, you may need to save the data in a plain file. Doing so is a simple task. To illustrate how to do it, we will reuse a transformation that was developed in the *Filtering Rows* section of Chapter 4, *Transforming Data*, and will send the data to a text file:

1. From the code developed in the last chapter, open the transformation that filtered places with more than three bedrooms or that accommodated more than four people. Save the transformation with a different name.
2. From the **Output** folder, drag and drop a **Text file output** step.
3. Create a hop from the **Filter rows** step (or the **Java Filter** step, depending on the step that you used) to the new step. When asked for the kind of hop, select **Main output of step**.
4. Double-click on the **Text file output** step.
    1. Under **Filename**, type the full path to the destination file. You can include variable names (for example, ${OUTPUT_FOLDER}/listing).

Note that there is a textbox for setting the extension of the output file. Therefore, you don't need to include it as a part of the filename.

5. Click on **Fields** and fill in the grid, as shown in the following screenshot:

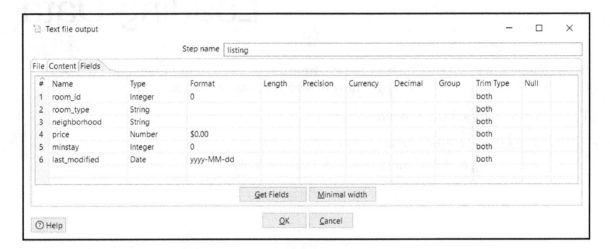

Configuring fields for an output file

6. Close the window, save the transformation, and run it.
7. Look at the **Step Metrics** in the **Execution Results** window. The Output column shows the number of rows sent to the file:

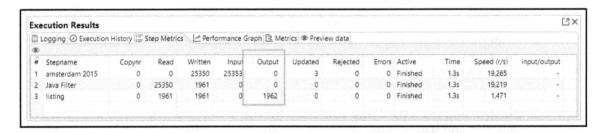

Step metrics

8. Browse your system to look for the output file. It should be in the indicated path, and its content should be as follows:

```
room_id;room_type;neighborhood;price;minstay;last_modified
22315;Entire home/apt;Oud Oost;$143.00;3;2015-01-19
25488;Entire home/apt;Oostelijk Havengebied / Indische
Buurt;$171.00;4;2015-01-19
44535;Private room;Slotervaart;$178.00;2;2015-01-19
47333;Entire home/apt;Centrum West;$193.00;3;2015-01-19
49552;Entire home/apt;Centrum West;$428.00;1;2015-01-19
50570;Entire home/apt;Bos en Lommer;$113.00;3;2015-01-19
...
```

As you can see, sending all (or a part) of a dataset to a file is really simple. We will highlight some details on the configuration of the **Text file output** step as follows:

- In the example, we used the default settings, but it's possible to customize the format (for example, changing the separator). You can do so in the **Content** tab.
- You can send all, or just a subset of, the fields coming into the step in the file. Also, the fields can be in any order, but you cannot rename them here. The headers in the file will match the field names in the dataset.

> If you want different names in the header of a file, you can set them by using a **Select values** step just before the **Text file output** step.

- While sending the data to a file, you can specify the format to apply to the fields. As an example, we added a dollar sign to the price, and we cut the time part of the timestamp.
- By default, the **Text file output** step generates files with `.txt` extensions, but you can change it to any other extension (for example, `.csv` or `.log`).

If you want to generate a spreadsheet, you will need a different step; you can use the **Microsoft Excel Output** step or the **Microsoft Excel Writer** step. With the first one, you generate `.xls` files, while the latter allows you to generate either `.xls` or `.xlsx` files. No matter which step you choose, the basic configuration is quite similar to the configuration for the **Text file output** step. Besides, these two steps also offer formatting options and the possibility to set the sheet names where the data should be saved.

> In order to understand the differences between these two steps, and to find out more details on how to configure them, please refer to the corresponding documentation.

Inserting and updating data in database tables

The dataset that you create in PDI can be inserted into tables, or can be used to update existing data. In this section, you will learn how to perform these two kinds of operation. For the tutorials, we will use the Sports database that we used in the previous chapters.

Inserting data

In order to insert new data into a table in a relational database, PDI has a couple of steps, the **Table output** step being the simplest option. In this case, we will read a file with information about new injuries and insert it into the `injuries_phases` table by using this step. The file is available with the bundle material for this chapter, and it looks as follows:

```
person_id;injury_type;injury_side;injury_date
812;elbow;left;2018-05-19
813;shoulder;left;2018-05-15
119;calf;both;2018-05-20
370;wrist;;2018-05-08
241;other-excused;;2018-05-26
790;shoulder;;2018-06-30
941;knee;right;2018-07-01
151;knee;right;2018-07-11
```

The instructions for inserting the file are as follows:

1. Create a transformation, and use a **Text file input** step to read the file with the new injuries. As in other exercises, feel free to create your own data instead.
2. From the **Output** folder, drag and drop an **Table output** step. Create a hop from the **Text file input** step to this one.
3. Double-click on the **Table output** step. In the **Connection** option, select the Sports database connection.

 If you didn't share the connection when you created it in Chapter 3, *Extracting Data*, you will have to create it again.

4. As the **Target table**, type `injury_phases`. Alternatively, you can click on **Browse...** and select the name from the list of available tables.

5. Check the **Specify database fields** option, and then select the **Database fields** tab.

6. Fill in the grid, as shown in the following screenshot:

Mapping fields in a Table output step

You can fill the grid in manually, but you can also use the **Get fields** button that will fill in the grid with the stream fieldnames, saving some editing time. There is also the **Enter field mapping** option, which allows you to define the mapping between the fields in your dataset and the columns in the destination table.

7. Close the window.
8. Save the transformation, and run it.
9. Look at the **Step Metrics** in the **Execution Results** window. The **Output** column shows the rows sent to the database:

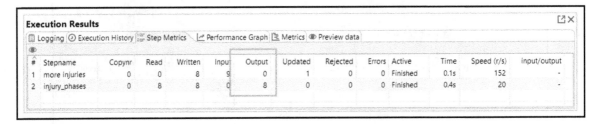

Step Metrics

10. Open the **Database Explorer,** or use the software of your choice, and run the following code:

```
SELECT * FROM injury_phases WHERE start_date_time > '2018-01-01'
```

11. As a result, you should get the rows that we just inserted (the rows coming from the file).

Updating data

Now, suppose that we have a similar file, but this time, there is a comment related to the injury:

```
person_id;injury_type;injury_side;injury_date;comment
812;elbow;left;2018-05-19;Season 2018
813;shoulder;left;2018-05-15;playing football
141;other-excused;;2018-05-26;serious injury
241;other-excused;;2018-05-26;serious injury
```

In this case, if the injury exists in the Injuries table, we want to update the comment:

1. Create a new transformation and use it to read the `more_injuries_with_comments.txt` file.
2. From the **Output** folder, drag and drop an **Update** step. Create a hop from the **Text file input** step to this one.
3. Double-click on the **Update** step. In the **Connection** option, select the `Sports` database connection.
4. As the **Target table**, type `injury_phases`.
5. Fill in the grid, as shown in the following screenshot:

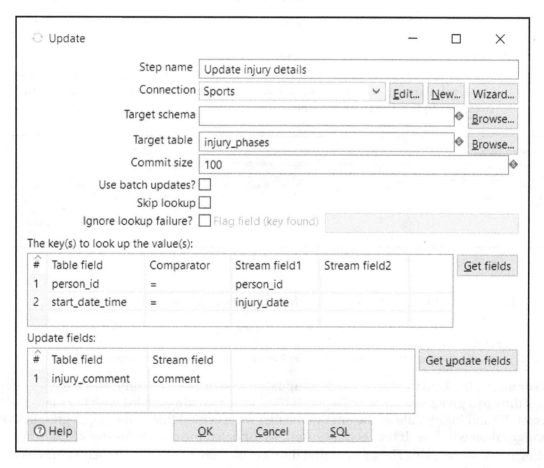

Configuring an Update step

6. From the **Utility** folder, drag and drop a **Write to log** step.

7. Create a hop from the **Update** step to the **Write to log** step. When asked for the kind of hop, select **Error handling of step**. Your transformation will look as follows:

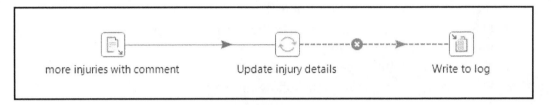

more injuries with comment   Update injury details   Write to log

Designing a transformation

8. Save the transformation, and run it.

9. Look at the **Step Metrics**. The **Update** step effectively updated three rows (see the **Updated** column). The fourth row was rejected (see the **Rejected** column) and sent to the **Write to log** step:

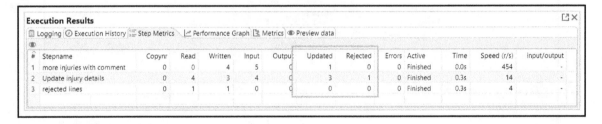

Execution Results

#	Stepname	Copynr	Read	Written	Input	Output	Updated	Rejected	Errors	Active	Time	Speed (r/s)	input/output
1	more injuries with comment	0	0	4	5	0	1	0	0	Finished	0.0s	454	-
2	Update injury details	0	4	3	4	0	3	1	0	Finished	0.3s	14	-
3	rejected lines	0	1	1	0	0	0	0	0	Finished	0.3s	4	-

Step Metrics

10. Run the following query to confirm that three rows where updated:

```
SELECT person_id, injury_type, injury_comment
FROM injury_phases
WHERE start_date_time > '2018-01-01' AND injury_comment is not null
```

In summary, the **Update** step is used for updating one or more columns in a table, according to a given key. In our case, we looked for an existing record with the same person ID and injury date as the ones in the file; we specified this in the upper grid, in the configuration window. If the record existed, we updated the comment—we did this by filling in the lower grid. The records that didn't exist were rejected, and their values were printed to the log.

Handling errors

In the previous example, we knew that the injury didn't exist in the destination table, but that is not the only possible error when trying to update a table. Let's refine our transformation a bit, as follows:

1. Right-click on the **Update** step and select **Error Handling....**
2. In the window that shows up, look for the **Error descriptions fieldname** textbox, and fill it in with the text `error_description`.
3. Close the window.
4. Run the transformation again. This time, no row is updated, as we already updated the comment the first time we ran the transformation.
5. If you look at the **Logging** window, you will see the details of the rejected row, including a new field with the description of the error that caused the rejection:

```
... - rejected lines.0 - ------------> Linenr 1--------------------
... - rejected lines.0 - person_id = 141
... - rejected lines.0 - injury_type = other-excused
... - rejected lines.0 - injury_side = null
... - rejected lines.0 - injury_date = 2018-05-26
... - rejected lines.0 - comment = serious injury
... - rejected lines.0 - error_description = Entry to update with
following key could not be found: [141], [2018-05-26]
... - rejected lines.0 -
... - rejected lines.0 - ====================
```

If, instead of rejecting the row, you want to insert the whole row with data about a new injury, you can use the **Insert/Update** step. This step, as the name implies, inserts new rows or updates the rows that already exist in the table.

 We just learn to capture errors when they occur in an **Update** step. For capturing errors caused in a different step, you proceed in the same way. You redirect the rejected rows to an alternative stream, and optionally, you add fields describing the error.

Loading a datamart

Aside from performing CRUD operations, PDI can be used to load datamarts. In order to demonstrate how PDI can help you to do so, we will populate a very simple datamart.

This is just a quick overview of the subject. We assume that you have at least a basic understanding of datawarehouse concepts (for example, dimensions, time dimensions, SCD, and fact tables).

The source data will be the Sports database. We will have a simple fact table and just three dimensions, as shown in the next diagram:

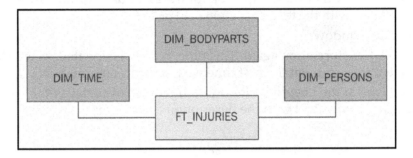

Injuries datamart

The fact table will keep track of the injuries suffered by sport players. This fact table will have just one measure: the quantity of injuries.

The dimensions involved in this datamart will be as follows:

- A time dimension, for the injury date
- A body parts dimension, with the name of the injured body part
- A person dimension, with the name of the injured player:

By loading this simple model, you will get a synopsis of the steps that PDI offers to build a datamart.

First, we will load the classical time dimension. Then, we will load the rest of the dimensions, and finally, we will load the fact table.

Before proceeding, download the code for the chapter and run the datamart.sql script, which will create the tables for the datamart.

Loading a time dimension

As mentioned previously, we will start by loading the time dimension. In order to keep the exercise simple, we will populate a dimension with just a few attributes. The following is the DDL for the corresponding table:

```
CREATE TABLE DIM_TIME (
  dateid integer NOT NULL,
  year integer NOT NULL,
  month smallint NOT NULL,
  day smallint NOT NULL,
  week_day smallint NOT NULL,
  week_day_desc CHAR(10) NOT NULL,
  month_desc CHAR(10) NOT NULL,
  PRIMARY KEY (dateid)
);
```

We will create a transformation that generates a dataset with 1,000 days (that is, 1,000 rows) and loads that data into the time dimension:

1. Create a transformation.
2. From the **Input** folder, drag and drop a **Generate Rows** step.
3. Use the **Generate Rows** step to generate a dataset with a single row and a single field containing the starting date: 2018-01-01. Use the following screenshot as a reference:

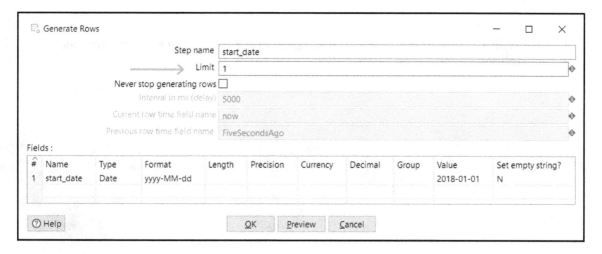

Generating a dataset

4. From the **Utility** folder, drag and drop a **Clone row** step. Create a hop from the **Generate row** step to this step.

5. Double-click on the **Clone row** step and set the number of clones (in the **Nr clones** textbox) to 999. As the entry implies, this will cause PDI to create 999 copies of the single row.

6. Also, check the **Add clone num to output?** checkbox, and, in the **Clone num field**, type delta.

7. Close the **Clone row** configuration window.

8. Next, add a **Calculator** step, and use it to create a field that will be the sum of the starting date plus the delta field:

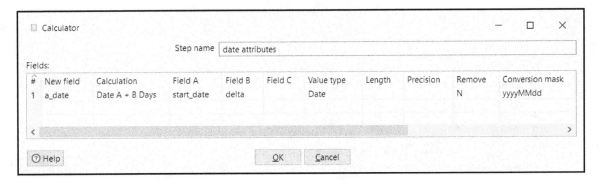

Creating a field with a Calculator

9. Close the window.

10. With the **Calculator** selected, run a preview. You will see a list of dates, as follows:

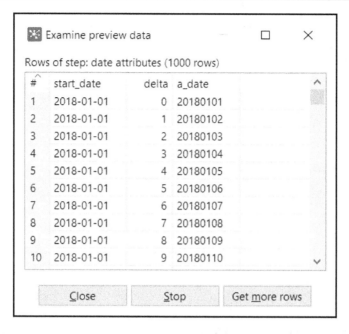

Previewing some dates

The dataset that we just created is the base for the time dimension. From this point, you can start to add all of the different attributes. In our dimension, we will just add a few of them:

1. Double-click on the **Calculator** step and add the following fields—year, month, day, and week_day:

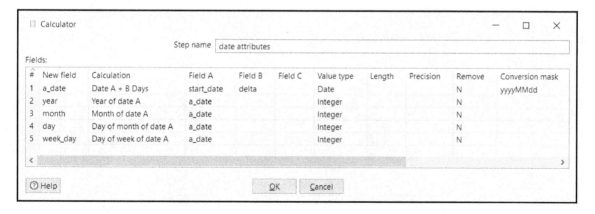

Configuring a Calculator

2. Now, we will add descriptions for the `month` and the `week_day`.

3. From the **Transform** folder, add two **Value Mapper** steps to the work area, and link them at the end of the stream. So far, you should have the following:

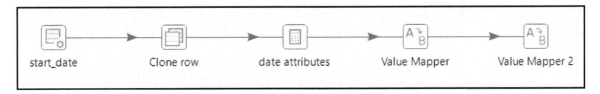

Designing a transformation

4. Double-click on the first **Value Mapper** step, and configure it as follows:

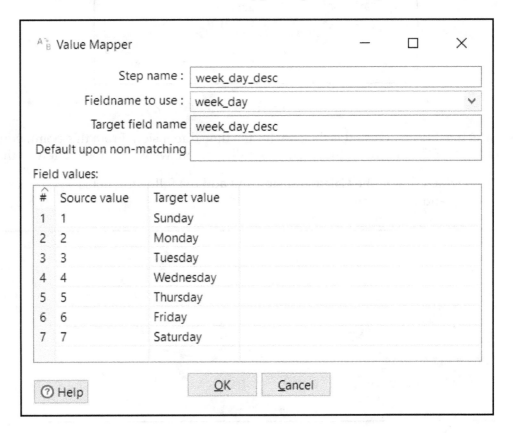

Configuring a Value Mapper step

5. In a similar way, configure the second **Value Mapper** step to create the field `month_desc`, with the names of the months. For **Fieldname to use:** select `month`, and as the **Target field name**, type `month_desc`. Then, fill in the grid with the twelve month names.

6. With the last step selected, run a preview. You will see the following:

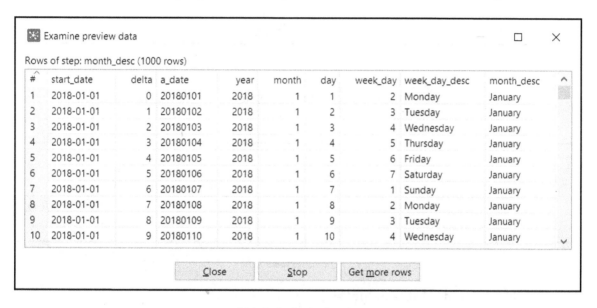

Previewing data for a time dimension

Before sending the data to the table, we will convert the date (which has a Date type) to a numeric field, in order to use it as the key in our dimension. As an example, suppose that we want the date `2018-01-01` to be converted to the number `20180101`. To do the conversion, we will first convert the field to a `String`, and then to an `Integer`.

Internally, the dates are stored as the number of milliseconds since January 1, 1970, 00:00:00 GMT. Therefore, if you convert a Date to an Integer without converting it to a String first, the final result will be the number of miliseconds converted to the Number datatype.

7. Next, add a **Select values** step, and use it to do the first conversion, as follows:

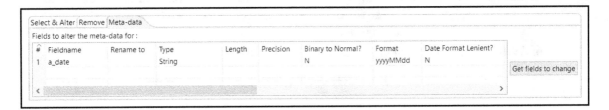

Changing metadata

8. After that, add another **Select values** step, and use it to do the second conversion, as follows:

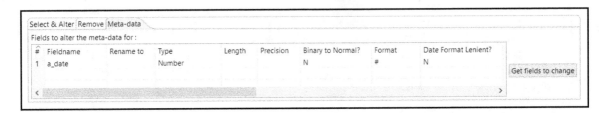

Changing metadata

9. Finally, add a **Table output** step.
10. Double-click on the step. Click on **New...** to create the connection for the datamart.
11. Create the connection to the datamart database and name it sample_dw.
12. Click on **OK**. The new connection will automatically be selected as the value for the **Connection** textbox.
13. As the **Target table,** select or type dim_time. Check the options **Truncate table** and **Specify database fields**.

14. Select the **Database fields** tab and fill in the grid, as shown in the following screenshot:

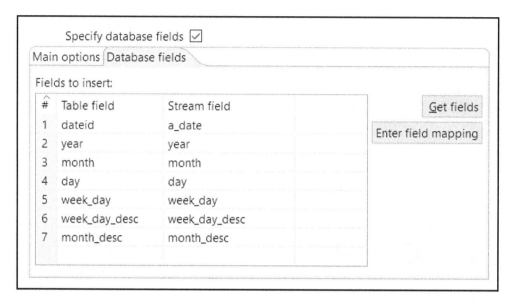

Mapping fields

15. Close the window, save the transformation, and run it.
16. Explore the database and run a SELECT statement over the time dimension. You will see the data that was just created.

The preceding transformation is just a starting point for loading a time dimension. You can modify it in several ways; for example, by adding more time attributes, generating more dates, or localizing the names (for instance, the month names or the weekday names).

Before proceeding, make sure to share the new connection. Right-click on the sample_dw database connection and click on **Share**. Now, you won't have to create it again in future transformations.

Loading other kinds of dimensions

In this subsection, we will load two dimensions: BODYPARTS and PERSONS. Let's start with the first one, which is the simplest.

Loading a dimension with a combination lookup/update step

The BODYPARTS dimension is meant to hold the name of the body part where the injury occurred. This table has no corresponding table in the source database. Because of that, there is no business key. The content is just a list of the different body parts and a surrogate key. The following is the DDL for the dimension table:

```
CREATE TABLE DIM_BODYPARTS (
  id integer NOT NULL,
  bodypart CHAR(50) NOT NULL,
  PRIMARY KEY (id)
);
```

Loading a dimension like this one is simple:

1. Create a transformation.
2. Drag and drop a **Table input** step. We will use it to get the data to load into the table.
3. Double-click on the step. As the **Connection**, select Sports. In the **SQL** box, type the following query:

   ```
   SELECT DISTINCT injury_type FROM injury_phases
   ```

4. Run a preview to make sure that you have the expected data.
5. Close the window.
6. From the **Data Warehouse** folder, drag and drop a **Combination lookup/update** step.
7. Create a hop from the **Table input** step to this new step.
8. Double-click on the **Combination lookup/update** step, and configure it as follows:

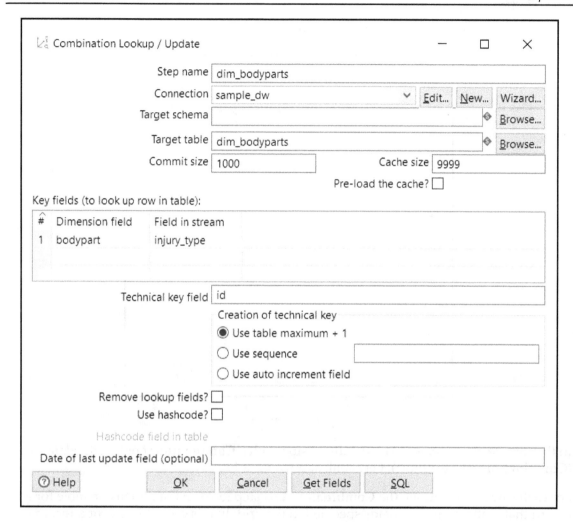

Configuring a Combination L/U step

9. Close the window and save the transformation.
10. Run the transformation. This will cause the dimension table to be loaded.
11. In the **View** tab, right-click on the **sample_dw** connection, open the **Database Explorer**, and run the following code:

```
SELECT * FROM dim_bodyparts
```

12. You should see the following result:

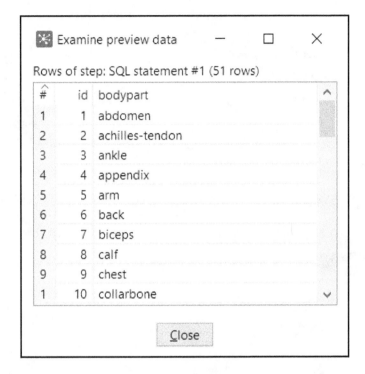

Previewing dimension data

In this simple example, we loaded a dimension with a **Combination Lookup/Update** step (**Combination L/U**, for short). Let's look at how it works.

For each row in the dataset, the **Combination L/U** step looks in the dimension table for a record that matches the key fields specified in the grid. In this case, it looks for a record where the column `bodypart` is equal to the value of the `injury_type` field. If the row doesn't exist, the step generates a new surrogate key, the **Technical key field**, and inserts a row with the key fields and the generated surrogate key.

Whether the row exists or not, the step returns the surrogate key and adds it to the main dataset. You can verify this by inspecting the output metadata of the step.

 The **Combination Lookup/Update** step can be used to load dimensions like the one in this example, and also to load Junk dimensions, mini dimensions, and any Type I SCD; that is, dimensions for which you are not interested in keeping historical values.

Loading a dimension with a dimension lookup/update step

The PERSONS dimension is meant to hold the names of the players. The main difference, as compared to the previous dimension, is that this one has a corresponding table in the source database. The following is the DDL for the dimension table:

```
CREATE TABLE DIM_PERSONS (
  id integer NOT NULL,
  first_name CHAR(25) NOT NULL DEFAULT 'N/A',
  last_name CHAR(25) NOT NULL DEFAULT 'N/A',
  entity_id integer NOT NULL DEFAULT 0,
  version integer,
  date_from TIMESTAMP,
  date_to TIMESTAMP,
  PRIMARY KEY (id)
);
```

In this table, the id is the surrogate key, while the entity_id corresponds to the business key.

The following instructions describe how to load the table:

1. Create a transformation.
2. Drag a **Table input** step into the work area, and use it to get the full list of players. In order to do so, select the Sports database connection and type the following query:

   ```
   SELECT p.id as person_id
     , coalesce(d.first_name, 'N/A') as first_name
     , coalesce(d.last_name, 'N/A') as last_name
   FROM persons p
   JOIN display_names d ON p.id = d.id
   AND d.entity_type = 'persons'
   ```

3. From the **Data Warehouse** folder, drag and drop a **Dimension lookup/update** step.
4. Create a hop from the **Table input** step to this new step.
5. Double-click on the **Dimension lookup/update** step. As the **Connection**, select the sample_dw option. As the **Target table**, select or type dim_persons.

6. Fill in the **Keys** tab of the grid, as shown in the following screenshot:

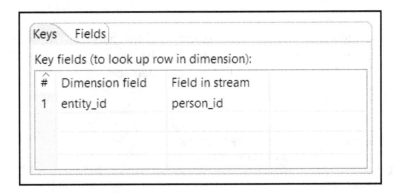

Keys tab in a Dimension L/U step

7. As the **Technical key field**, select id.
8. Select the **Fields** tab and fill in the grid as follows:

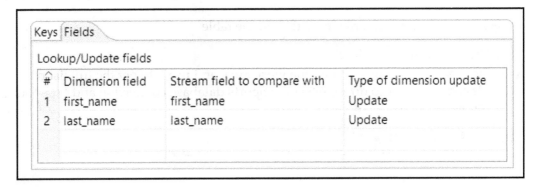

Fields tab in a Dimension L/U step

9. Close the window and save the transformation.
10. Run the transformation. This will cause the dimension table to be loaded.
11. In the **View** tab of Spoon, right-click on the sample_dw connection and select **Explore** to open the Database Explorer.
12. Look for the dim_persons table, right-click on it, and select **Preview first 100**. You should see the following:

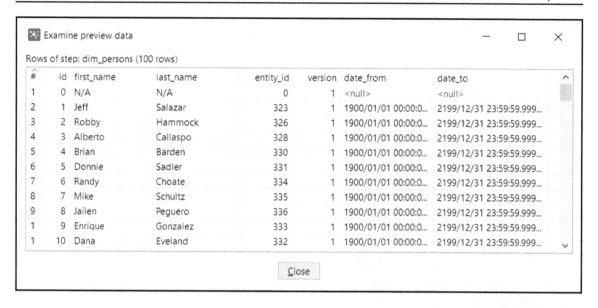

Previewing dimension data

Let's look at how the **Dimension Lookup/Update** step works in our transformation.

For each row, it looks for a record where the business key (the `entity_id` field) matches the `person_id` in the dataset. If it finds it, it updates the `first_name` and `last_name` fields. If the record doesn't exist, it generates a surrogate key (the `technical key` field) and inserts a new record with the data provided.

In general, the **Dimension Lookup/Update** step (Dimension L/U, for short) is meant to load SCDs, and is prepared to keep a history of the changes. Even if you don't want to keep the history, as in our example, the step requires that the dimension table has a field for the version, and two fields for a range of dates:

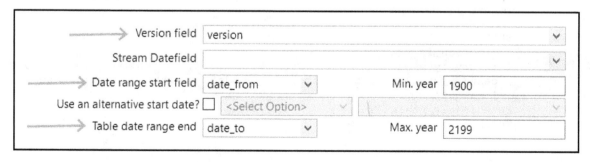

Fields for keeping history

As shown in the preceding screenshot, the default names for the fields are
`version`, `date_from`, and `date_to`. This explains why we created those extra fields in the
table.

In the tutorial, we used the Dimension L/U step to load a Type I SCD, but the step is
prepared to load a Type II SCD in a very custom fashion. For example, the step can be used
to keep the history selectively, depending on the fields that change.

 Loading a Type II SCD is out of the scope of this book. If you want to
learn more about the full use and configuration of a **Dimension L/U** step
for loading a Type II SCD, you can read the book *Learning Pentaho Data
Integration 8 CE*, by Packt Publishing.

Loading a fact table

We already have the dimension tables loaded. It's time to load the fact table. The following
is the DDL for the `Injuries` fact table:

```
CREATE TABLE FT_INJURIES (
  date integer NOT NULL,
  id_bodypart integer NOT NULL,
  id_person integer NOT NULL,
  quantity integer DEFAULT 0 NOT NULL
  );
```

This is a cumulative fact table that we will load in an incremental way. Suppose that the
fact table is already loaded with injuries having occurred up until `2007-07-31`. Now, we
have to load the new data, as follows:

1. Create a transformation, and drag in a **Table input** step.
2. Double-click on the step. Select the **Sports** connection. As the **SQL**, type the
   following statement:

   ```
   SELECT
     i.person_id
   , injury_type
   , cast(to_char(start_date_time, 'yyyymmdd') as int) as injury_date
   , 1 as qty
   FROM injury_phases i
   WHERE start_date_time > '2007-07-31'
   ```

The date in the WHERE clause is hardcoded for the purposes of demonstration. In a real scenario, you will use a variable instead.

3. Run a preview to verify that the data is as expected.
4. Close the window.
5. The preceding query contains the business keys for both the person and the body part. We have to get the surrogate keys. We can do so with a **Database lookup** step, which you learned how to use in the last chapter.
6. From the **Lookup** folder, drag and drop two **Database lookup** steps, and link the steps, as shown in the following diagram. When asked for the kind of hop, select **Main output of step:**

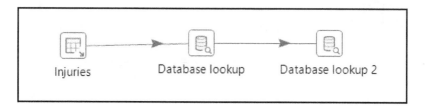

Designing a transformation

7. Double-click on the first **Database lookup** step. We will use it to get the surrogate key for the PERSONS dimension.
8. As the **Connection**, select sample_dw. As the **Lookup table**, select or type dim_persons. Fill in the grids as follows:

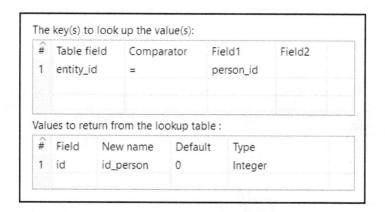

The key(s) to look up the value(s):

#	Table field	Comparator	Field1	Field2
1	entity_id	=	person_id	

Values to return from the lookup table :

#	Field	New name	Default	Type
1	id	id_person	0	Integer

Configuring a Database lookup step

9. Close the window.

10. Now, double-click on the second **Database lookup** step. This step will be used to get the surrogate key for the BODYPARTS dimension.

11. As the **Connection**, select sample_dw. As the **Lookup table**, select or type dim_bodyparts. Fill in the grids as follows:

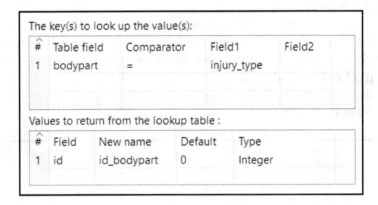

The key(s) to look up the value(s):

#	Table field	Comparator	Field1	Field2
1	bodypart	=	injury_type	

Values to return from the lookup table :

#	Field	New name	Default	Type
1	id	id_bodypart	0	Integer

Configuring a Database lookup step

12. Close the window.

13. With the last step selected, run a preview. You will see the following:

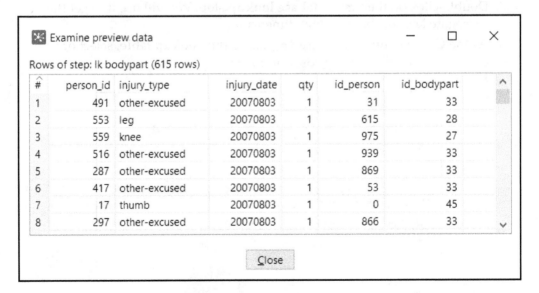

Examine preview data — □ ×

Rows of step: lk bodypart (615 rows)

#	person_id	injury_type	injury_date	qty	id_person	id_bodypart
1	491	other-excused	20070803	1	31	33
2	553	leg	20070803	1	615	28
3	559	knee	20070803	1	975	27
4	516	other-excused	20070803	1	939	33
5	287	other-excused	20070803	1	869	33
6	417	other-excused	20070803	1	53	33
7	17	thumb	20070803	1	0	45
8	297	other-excused	20070803	1	866	33

Close

Previewing a transformation

14. Close the window.
15. Finally, add a **Table output** step.
16. Double-click on the step. As the **Connection**, select `sample_dw`. As the **Target table**, select or type `ft_injuries`. Check the option **Specify database fields**.
17. Select the **Database fields** tab and fill in the grid as follows:

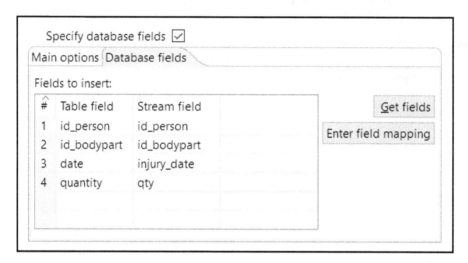

Mapping fields

18. Close the window, save the transformation, and run it.
19. Explore the database and run a `SELECT` statement to query the fact table. You will see how the previewed data was inserted.

In this tutorial, we assumed that the dimensions were already loaded. Alternatively, we can load the dimensions at the same time that the fact is being loaded. Instead of using a **Database lookup** step, we can use the same step that we used when we loaded the dimensions.

> Both the **Combination L/U** step and the **Dimension L/U** step return the corresponding surrogate keys and add them to the main stream. Therefore, the steps can be used for both updating the dimensions and looking up a surrogate key at the same time.

Summary

In this chapter, you learned how to send data to files (specifically, plain files and spreadsheets). Then, you learned how to perform `insert` and `update` operations on relational databases. You also learned how to handle any errors that may occur. Finally, you were briefly introduced to using PDI to load datamarts, including time dimensions, other kinds of dimensions, and fact tables.

You already have the basic knowledge required for dealing with data in PDI. In the next chapter, you will learn how to orchestrate all of your work, including the work you have done so far, through the use of PDI jobs.

Orchestrating Your Work

6

In this chapter, you will learn how to organize your work with PDI jobs. By the end of the chapter, you will be able to use PDI jobs to sequence tasks, dealing with files, sending emails, and other useful tasks.

The following topics will be covered in this chapter:

- Understanding the purpose of PDI jobs
- Designing and running jobs
- Combining the execution of jobs and transformations
- Running jobs with the Kitchen utility

Understanding the purpose of PDI jobs

There are two main artifacts in PDI: **transformations** and **jobs**. While transformations deal mainly with data, jobs deal with tasks or processes. With a job, you organize a list of tasks by indicating the order of execution and deciding whether the execution should depend on certain conditions. Consider the following sample PDI job:

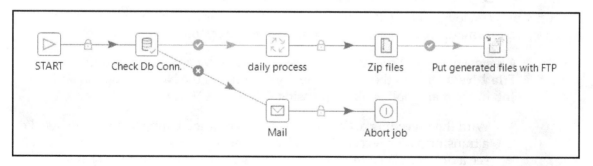

Sample PDI job

One of the good things about PDI is that by simply taking a look at the graphical representation of a job or a transformation in Spoon, it is quite easy to deduce its general purpose. In this example, we can see that the sample job checks some database connections. If everything is okay, it executes a daily process. Then, it compress some files in a ZIP format, putting the files in a remote server with FTP. If there is a problem with the database connection, the job sends an email and aborts.

Let's list some more examples of PDI jobs, as follows:

- Download a list of files from a server. Validate the data that is stored in the files, then import the values into a table in a database.
- Create a backup of files found in a given folder. If something goes wrong, send an email with the details.
- Load a datamart; that is, update the dimensions, and then load the newest data into the fact tables.
- Run some scripts that clean data in a database. Generate a log with the results.

In the next sections, you will learn how to create these kinds of processes.

Designing and running jobs

In this section, you will learn the basics involved in jobs. First, you will create and run a very simple job, in order to get familiar with the process. Then, you will learn how to sequence tasks; finally, you will be guided into the world of job entry.

Creating and running a simple job

To create and run jobs, you use the same tool that is used for creating, previewing, and running transformations: **Spoon**. Let's look at how to use Spoon to work with jobs:

1. Create a new job. You can do so in several ways: by accessing the option **File | New | Job** in the main menu, by clicking on the **New file** option and then **Job** in the main toolbar, or by pressing *Ctrl + Alt + N*.

   With the preceding action, you will see a new job template, which looks like a transformation, except for the icon at the top of the work area. You will also see a different **Design** tree, which contains **job entries** instead of steps.

2. From the **General** folder, drag a **START** entry to the canvas.

The **START** entry is mandatory in every job, and it has to be the first entry in the sequence.

3. From the **Utility** folder, drag a **Ping a host** entry.
4. Create a hop from the **START** entry to this new entry. You create hops in the same way that you do so when designing a transformation. For example, you can select the origin and destination entries, then right-click and select **New Hop....**

Alternatively, you can create a hop by using the middle mouse button, or the tiny toolbars.

5. Double-click on the **Ping a host** entry. In the **Host name/IP:** textbox, type `google.com`.

6. Close the window and save the job. You will see the following:

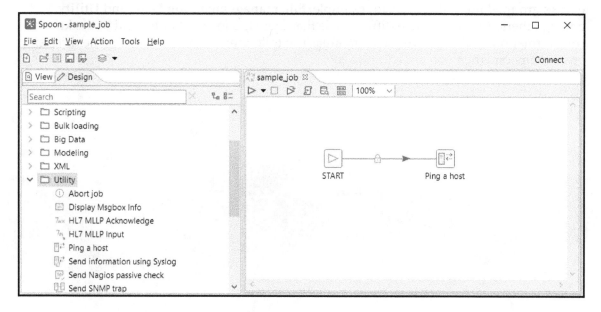

Simple job

7. Run the job. You can do so by navigating to **Action** | **Run** in the main menu, by selecting the first icon in the menu above the job area, or by pressing *F9*.

8. Under **Log level:**, select `Detailed`.

9. Click on **Run**.

10. While the job is running, you will see how the log is being generated in the **Logging** tab of the **Execution Results** window. After the execution, you will see something like the following:

```
... - Spoon - Starting job...
... - sample_job - Start of job execution
... - START - Starting job entry
... - sample_job - Starting entry [Ping a host]
... - Ping a host - Starting job entry
...
... - Ping a host - Host [google.com] is reachable.
... - sample_job - Finished job entry [Ping a host] (result=
    [true])
... - sample_job - Job execution finished
... - Spoon - Job has ended.
```

This simple tutorial should be enough for you to understand how to create and run a job, and how this task differs from working with transformations. The first thing that we noted was that the **Design** tree was different. When you work with jobs, this tree shows job entries grouped into categories, for example, **File management**, **Big Data**, and **Utility**, among others. Another visible difference is that there is a job toolbar instead of the known transformation toolbar above the work area. The following screenshot depicts the different areas in Spoon when you are editing a job:

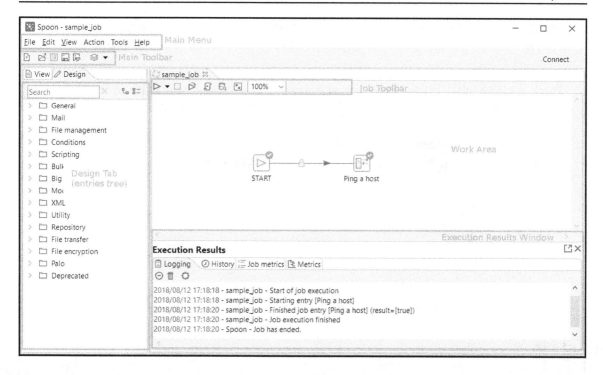

Spoon Interface

When you run a job, the **Logging** tab in the **Execution Results** window shows the log with different levels of detail, just as it does when you run a transformation. There is also a **Job metrics** tab, analogous to the **Step Metrics** tab, which will be explained later.

Finally, as you aren't dealing with data, but with tasks, it makes no sense to have preview options when working with jobs.

Understanding the results of execution

One thing that you may have noticed is that after running the job, the entries were marked with a green tick, as shown in the following diagram:

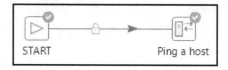

Ticks indicating the result of the execution

These ticks indicate that the entries ran successfully. In general, every single entry in a job ends with a result: **success** or **failure**. Let's perform a simple test to see the options, as follows:

1. Double-click on the **Ping a host** entry and change the host to an invalid one. Adding a special character will be enough; for instance, you can type `google.com@`.

2. Close the window, save the job, and run it.

3. This time, the **Ping a host** entry will be marked with a red cross. Also, if you look at the **Execution Result** window you will see how the log reports the error, also in a red font:

   ```
   Ping a host - ERROR (version 8.1.0.0-365, build 8.1.0.0-365 from
   2018-04-30 09.42.24 by buildguy) : We cannot ping the host
   google.com@
   ```

Now, click on the **Job metrics** tab; you will see the following:

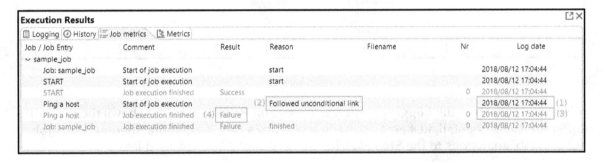

Job metrics

For each entry, you will see the following:

- The timestamp indicating when it started (**1**)
- The reason why it started (this information will make more sense in the next section) (**2**)
- The timestamp indicating when it ended (**3**)
- The result of the execution: success or failure (**4**)

The result of each entry can be used for sequencing tasks, as explained in the following section.

Sequencing tasks

In the preceding example, we had only two entries: a **START** entry (mandatory in every job) and a **Ping a host** entry. This job was deliberately simple, in order to demonstrate how to create and run a job. In the real world, jobs can have several linked entries, as shown in the following diagram:

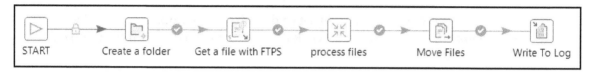

Sample job with many entries

This sample job was designed to run all of the entries in a row, but that's not always the case. As shown in the very first example in the chapter, the entries can also take alternative paths. Upon the success of an entry, you can take one way or another in the flow. The execution of every entry will depend on the result of the previous entry and the kind of hop that links them:

- An entry at the end of a green hop will execute whether the previous entry succeeded.
- An entry at the end of a red hop will execute whether the previous entry failed.
- An entry at the end of a gray hop will always execute, no matter the result of the previous entry.

 If you are looking at the screenshots in black and white, here is a hint: green hops are those with a tick icon in the middle, red hops are those with a cross, and gray hops are those with a lock icon.

Let's look at how you can design these alternative paths in a job:

1. Create a job and drag a **START** entry to the work area.
2. From the **File management** folder, drag a **Create a folder** entry, and create a link from the **START** entry to this new entry.
3. Double-click on the **Create a folder** entry. In the **Folder name** textbox, type ${NEW_FOLDER}, and close the window.

4. From the **Utility** folder, drag a **Write To Log** entry, and create a hop from the **Create a folder** entry toward it. The hop will be created in green, by default.

5. Double-click on the **Write To Log** entry. In the **Log subject** textbox, type `Folder created successfully`.

6. From the **Utility** folder, drag another **Write To Log** entry, and create a hop from the **Create a folder** entry toward it. This hop will be created in red.

 When you create a hop, PDI sets a default type of hop. If you need to change it, you can do so by clicking on the small icon. Each time you click on it, the type of hop changes.

7. Double-click on the **Write To Log** entry. In the **Log subject** textbox, type `The folder ${NEW_FOLDER} couldn't be created`. For the **Log message**, type `There was an error creating the folder. Verify and retry.`

8. Close the window. The job will look as follows:

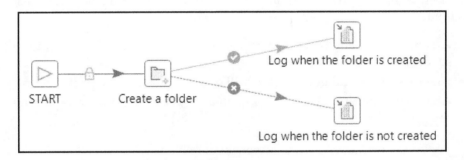

Sample job with alternative paths

9. Save the job, and press *F9* to run it.

10. Select the **Variables** tab and provide a value for the NEW_FOLDER variable. This should be a valid name for a new folder. The following screenshot shows an example:

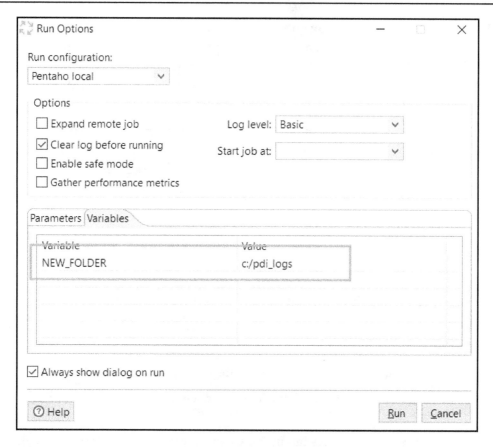

Providing values for a variable

11. Click on **Run**.

12. The folder will be created. The entries will be marked with the results of the execution, as follows:

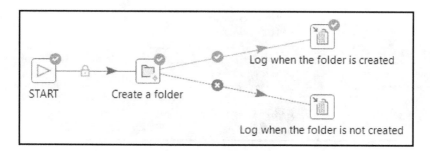

Executed job

13. The second **Write To Log** entry doesn't have a mark, as it didn't run.

14. Press *F9* to run the job again. This time, provide a value that is not proper for a folder (for example, `%%pdifolder`).

15. As a result, you will see that the **Create a folder** entry failed, and consequently, the second **Write To Log** entry was executed:

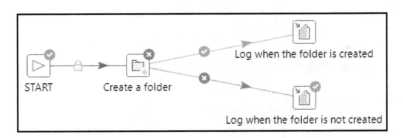

Job executed with errors

16. Also, in the **Logging** tab, you will see the error explained, as follows:

```
... - Create a folder - Unable to get VFS File object for filename
'%%pdifolder' : Invalid URI escape sequence "%%p".
```

You will also see the message written by the **Write To Log** entry, as follows:

```
... - The folder %%pdifolder couldn't be created - There was an
error creating the folder. Verify and retry.
```

Now, take a look at the **Job Metrics** tab in the **Execution Results** window. You will see the following details:

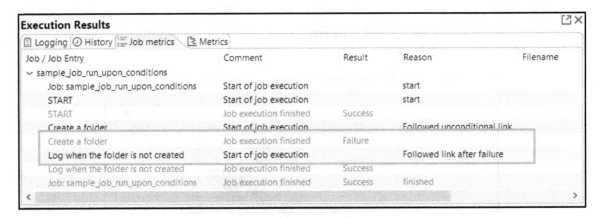

Job metrics

The result of the **Create a folder** entry was `Failure`. As a consequence, the reason for the second **Write To Log** being executed was `Followed link after failure`.

Taking a tour of the job entries

As mentioned previously, when you are designing a job, there is a broad list of available job entries, organized in folders. Let's review the list, grouped by general purpose, as follows:

- **Working with files**: In a job, you can manage files in several ways; you can create folders, move files, delete files, zip or unzip files, transfer files to and from remote servers, and more. You will find the corresponding entries in the following entry folders: `File management`, `File encryption`, and `File transfer`.

- **Interacting with databases**: You have already learned how to work with databases in a transformation, where you deal with data. With jobs, you have the option to perform more general tasks; for example, you can verify database connections, verify whether a table contains certain data, and run DDL scripts. You will find entries for doing such tasks inside of the following folders: `Conditions`, `Scripting` (**SQL entry**), `Bulk loading`, and `Big Data` (`Sqoop Export` and `Sqoop Import`).

- **Verifying conditions to change the flow of execution**: Aside from checking the result of an entry (success or failure), you can create a flow of tasks, based on the result of evaluating a condition. Examples of these conditions include checking whether a file exists, evaluating file metrics, and comparing the value of a variable with an expected value. Once the condition is evaluated, you can take one way or another in the flow depending on the result of the evaluation. There are entries devoted to this, and, as you may have guessed, all of them are inside of the **Conditions** folder.

- **Dealing with big data**: There is a dedicated folder for working with big data tools and frameworks. In particular, one of the first big data technologies integrated with PDI was **Hadoop**. In a PDI job, you can run Hadoop jobs, copy files from and to the Hadoop filesystem, and run the Sqoop tool for importing and exporting data from and to HDFS.

 The preceding list is not intended to be a full list of entries and categories, but rather an overview of the main (or most useful) ones.

As you already know, using an entry is just a matter of linking it as a part of your flow and configuring the behavior in its configuration window. As an example, the next subsection describes how to use the **Mail** entry to send an email, which is a very common requirement.

Sending emails

One of the tasks that you can do with a job is sending emails. In this section, we will create a very basic job, so that you can learn how to perform this task; later in the chapter, we will use it in a practical example.

 For performing this exercise, you will need access to an SMTP server, and at least one valid account to play with. For demonstration purposes, we will create a job that uses Gmail's SMTP server.

The following are the instructions for sending an email with a PDI job:

1. Create a job and drag a **START** entry from the **General** folder.
2. From the **Mail** folder, drag a **Mail** entry. Create a hop from the **START** to the **Mail** entry.
3. Double-click on the **Mail** entry. In the **Addresses** tab, provide, at a minimum, the destination address and the sender's name and address.

 In order to send the email to more than a single destination, you can supply the list of email addresses, separated by semicolons.

4. Select the **Server** tab and fill in all of the fields related to the SMTP server. The following is an example, illustrating how to configure the tab for a Gmail account:

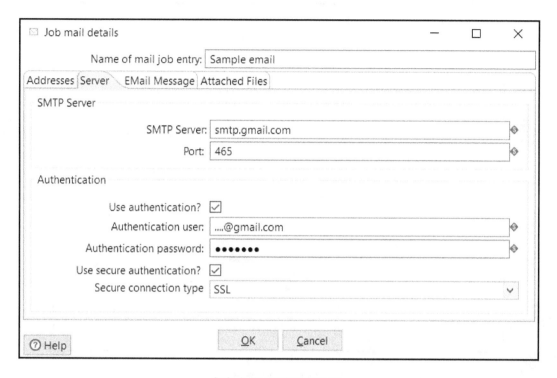

Configuring the server in a Mail job entry

5. Now, select the **EMail Message** tab, and select the **Only send comment in mail body?** checkbox.

6. In the **Message** box, type the subject and contents of the email, as shown in the following screenshot:

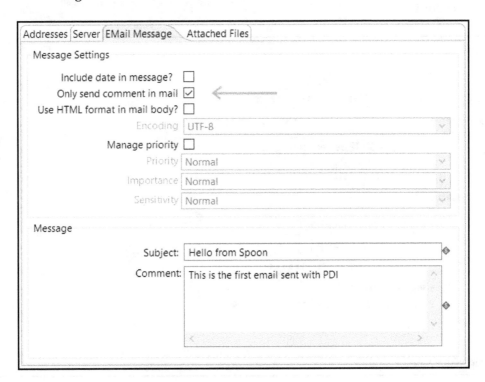

Configuring an email's content

7. Close the window and save the job.

8. Run the job. The email should be sent to the specified destination address.

As mentioned previously, the email that you send in a job can have several destinations. However, the mail itself is the same for everyone. If you need to send different emails at once, you can do so with a transformation. In that case, you will use the **Mail** step, which you will find inside of the **Utility** folder. Aside from the fact that the job sends a single email and the transformation can send multiple different emails at once, there is a difference between the way you configure the email with the **Mail** job entry and with the **Mail** step. As you just learned, the **Mail** job entry takes the required values (server configuration, addresses, and more) from variables or static text. On the other hand, in a **Mail** step, most of the values have to be defined as fields coming from previous steps.

While some entries are a bit complex in their configurations, you shouldn't have issues with using them. Even though there are some advanced concepts that are not covered here, the basic use of entries is, in general, quite intuitive. If you have doubts when experimenting with a new one, don't hesitate to browse the online documentation.

Combining the execution of jobs and transformations

In real projects, you don't run isolated transformations or jobs. Instead, you combine their execution, in order to create a flow of tasks. In particular, you can run jobs or transformations from a job, and you can also iterate the execution of transformations and jobs by simulating a loop. In this section, you will learn how to implement some of these combinations. The sample jobs and transformations will be related to the datamart introduced in Chapter 5, *Loading Data*.

Executing transformations from a job

To demonstrate how to execute a transformation from a job, we will create a job with the following purpose: it will find out the maximum date in the injuries fact table, and then it will load the fact table by using that date to filter the data to insert.

Before continuing, make sure that you delete the data inserted in the previous chapter from the Injuries fact table. This will allow you to follow the next exercises exactly as they are explained.

First, create a transformation that finds out the maximum date in the fact table, as follows:

1. Create a transformation.
2. Drag a **Table input** step into the work area.
3. Double-click on the step. As the **Connection**, select sample_dw.
4. In the **SQL** box, type the query that gets the maximum date: SELECT MAX(date) AS MAXDATE FROM ft_injuries.
5. Close the window.
6. From the **Job** folder, drag a **Set variables** step to the work area. We will use it to create a variable that holds the value for the maximum date.
7. Create a hop from the **Table input** to the **Set variables** step.

8. Double-click on the **Set variables** step, and configure it as follows:

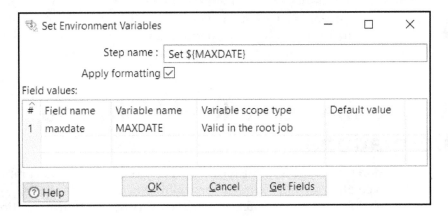

Configuring a Set variables step

9. Close the window. A warning message will appear. Close it; we will discuss it just after this tutorial.
10. Save the transformation with the name set_maxdate.ktr, in a folder named transformations.
11. Run the transformation, and look at the log. You will see that the variable was created as expected, as follows:

```
... - Set ${MAXDATE}.0 - Set variable MAXDATE to value [20080826]
```

Now, let's quickly adapt the transformation that loads the fact table. When we created that transformation, we used a fixed date. Now, we will use the MAX_DATE variable:

1. Open the transformation that loads the fact table.
2. Double-click on the **Table input** step.
3. Replace the WHERE statement with the hardcoded date with the following: WHERE start_date_time > '${MAXDATE}'.
4. Check the **Replace variables in script?** option, and close the window.
5. Save the transformation.

Finally, let's put it all together:

1. Create a new job.
2. From the **General** folder, drag a **START** entry and two **Transformation** job entries to the work area.

3. Link the entries, as shown in the following diagram:

Designing a job

1. Save the job in the same folder that contains the `transformations` folder.
2. Double-click on the first **Transformation** entry.
3. In the **Transformation:** textbox, type the path for the transformation that sets the variable. You may use variables like in the following example: `${Internal.Entry.Current.Directory}/transformations/set_maxdate.ktr`.

> Alternatively, you can browse and select the file by clicking on the **Browse...** button.

4. Close the window and double-click on the second **Transformation** entry.
5. In the **Transformation:** textbox, type the path for the transformation that loads the fact table; for example, `${Internal.Entry.Current.Directory}/transformations/fact_injuries.ktr`.
6. Close the window and save the job.
7. Run the job. In the log, you will see that eight rows were inserted - the same rows that we added to the Sports database in the last chapter:

```
... - fact injuries.0 - Finished processing (I=0, O=8, R=8, W=8,
    U=0, E=0)
```

8. Also, you can verify that the new injuries were added to the fact table by running the following query:

```
SELECT *
FROM ft_injuries
WHERE date > '20171231'
```

As show in the preceding example, running a transformation from a job is as simple as dragging the dedicated entry to the work area and providing the name and path of the transformation to run. Of course, there are several advanced settings; but, for simple tasks, this basic setting should be enough.

Creating user-defined Kettle variables

In the last exercise, you had the chance to learn a new way to define a variable. You calculated the value, and then you used a **Set variable** step to assign the value to a new variable. By setting the scope to **Valid in the root job**, you told PDI that the value should be visible in the root job (that is, the job that executes the transformation), and in all of the jobs and transformations called by this root job.

In general, you can define more than one variable with a single **Set variables** step, and each variable can have a different scope. The only restriction, as the warning message stated, is that the variable should not be used in the same transformation that creates it.

Nesting transformations and jobs

In the example developed in the previous section, you executed a transformation from a job. In the same way, you can execute a job from a job. The **subjob,** or inner job (that is, the job called by the main job), can also execute one or several subjobs or transformations, and so forth. To see a practical example of this, let's create a main job that loads the sample datamart by executing the different jobs and transformations that we have created so far.

First, let's create a job that loads all of the dimensions (with the exception of the TIME dimension, which is usually created once and never updated):

1. Create a new job.
2. Drag one **START** entry and two **Transformation** job entries to the work area, and link them in sequence.

3. Configure the **Transformation** entries to run the transformation that loads the BODY_PARTS and PERSON dimensions. The following screenshot depicts your final job:

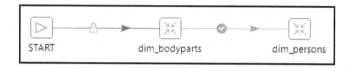

Job that loads dimensions

4. Save the job.

We already have a job that loads the injuries fact table. Now, let's create the main job, as follows:

1. Create a new job and save it in the same folder as the job created in the preceding steps.
2. From the **General** folder, drag one **START** entry and two **Job** entries into the work area. Link them in sequence.
3. Double-click on the first **Job** entry.
4. In the **Job:** textbox, type the path for the job that loads the dimensions. You may use variables; for example, ${Internal.Entry.Current.Directory}/load_dimensions.kjb.

The variable ${Internal.Entry.Current.Directory} will only have a value if the job that we are designing has been saved. Therefore, we have asked you to save it before configuring these entries.

5. Close the window and double-click on the second **Job** entry.
6. In the **Job:** textbox, type the path for the job that loads the fact table; for example, ${Internal.Entry.Current.Directory}/load_fact_injuries. kjb.
7. Close the window. You will see the following result:

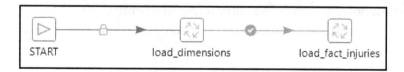

Job that loads a datamart

The only purpose of this job is to run the two subjobs in a row, avoiding running the subjobs separately. If any of the subjobs fail, the main job will abort. Let's add some more functionality. In the case of an error, we will send an email with the log attached, as follows:

1. Open the job, if you had closed it.
2. Double-click on the first **Job** entry.
3. Select the **Logging** tab, and configure it to generate a log with the details of the execution. Use the following screenshot as an example:

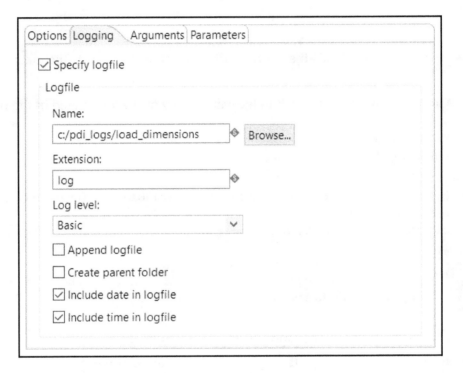

Configuring the log for a job

4. Close the window, and repeat the configuration for the other **Job** entry.
5. From the **Utility** folder, add a **Mail** entry to the job.
6. Create a hop from each **Job** entry to the **Mail** entry.
7. Make sure that the **Mail** entry is reached only if the jobs fail; that is, make the hops red.

8. Configure the **Mail** entry to send an email informing the user that there was an error while loading the datamart.

> If you need help configuring the entry, check the email tutorial in the Designing and Running Jobs section earlier in this chapter.

9. Before closing the **Mail** configuration window, select the **Attached Files** tab.
10. Check the **Attach file(s) to message?** option. The **Select file type:** list is enabled. In the list provided, select the **Log** option.
11. Close the window.
12. After the **Mail** entry, add an **Abort** entry. You will find it in the **Utility** folder.
13. Make sure that the **Abort** entry runs unconditionally; that is, make sure that the hop from the **Mail** entry to the **Abort** entry has the lock icon.
14. Save the job. The following diagram shows the final result:

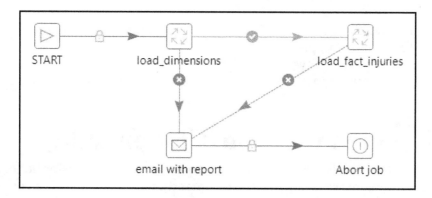

Job that loads a datamart and sends an email with a log

15. Run the job. If everything is okay, the datamart should be updated, and no email should be sent.
16. Now, introduce a deliberate error into any of the transformations. You could, for example, write a typo in any of the SQL queries.
17. Run the job again. This time, an email should be sent with the log attached. Also, the main job should abort after sending the email.

We just used an **Abort** entry, which, as the name implies, causes the job to abort. We will now explain why we need this entry. If one of the inner jobs fails, the execution follows the corresponding red hop—that is, the hop that goes towards the **Mail** entry. If the email is successfully sent, the main job will end with success as its final status. By adding the **Abort** entry, we force the job to end with an error, which will better represent the situation: there was an error in the main process, and we want the user to notice it.

 Note that the unconditional hop toward the **Abort** entry will force the job to abort, no matter what the result of the execution of the previous entry is (the **Mail** entry, in this case).

One step forward in the combination of PDI artifacts, is the possibility to run jobs and transformations in an iterative way. Suppose that you a list of people, files, codes, and so on. In case you need to run a transformation or a job once for each element in that list, you can do so by using the following steps: **Transformation Executor** or **Job Executor**, respectively, both located in the **Flow** steps folder. These steps have a rich set of configuration settings, which are worth exploring.

 For details about the use of the **Transformation Executor** and **Job Executor** steps, please refer to the PDI documentation at `https://help.pentaho.com/Documentation/8.1/Products/Data_Integration/Transformation_Step_Reference`.

Running jobs with the Kitchen utility

In `Chapter 2`, *Getting Familiar with Spoon*, you learned how to run transformations in production environments by using the `Pan` command-line utility. There is a counterpart tool for running jobs: the `Kitchen` command. Using `Kitchen` is no different than using `Pan`. The tool comes in two flavors: `Kitchen.bat` and `Kitchen.sh`, for use in a Windows or a Linux system, respectively. Let's review the different options. The simplest way to run a job is to indicate the full path of the `kjb` file. You do so with the following syntax:

```
Kitchen.bat /file=<kjb file name>
```

You can also use the following command:

```
Kitchen.sh /file=<kjb file name>
```

For example, if you want to load the datamart from the command line in Windows, you can do so by running the following command:

```
Kitchen.bat /file=c:/pdi/load_datamart.kjb
```

`Kitchen` can receive the same parameters that `Pan` does; the most common are as follows:

- `level`: This indicates the log level. The syntax for setting the log level is `/level:<log level>`, where the possible values for the level are `Nothing`, `Minimal`, `Error`, `Basic`, `Detailed`, `Debug`, and `Rowlevel`.
- `param`: This is used once for each parameter that you want to pass to the job. The syntax for providing a parameter is `/param:"<name of the named parameter>=<value for the parameter>"`.

For a full list of options for the `Kitchen` command, run `Kitchen.bat` or `Kitchen.sh` without parameters, and all of the options will be displayed.

Summary

In this chapter, you were introduced to PDI jobs, which, along with transformations, constitute the main artifacts of PDI.

First, you learned the purpose of jobs, and how they differ from PDI transformations. Through using Spoon, you learned how to design and run jobs. Then, through a series of tutorials, you worked with files, sent emails, generated logs, and more. Also, you learned how to combine the execution of jobs and transformations in different ways. Finally, you explored the `Kitchen` utility, used for running jobs from the command line.

This was the last chapter of this *Pentaho Data Integration Quick Start Guide*. Having read all of these pages, I hope that you feel familiar with the tool and are now confident enough to create your first projects and eager to learn more about PDI.

Other Books You May Enjoy

If you enjoyed this book, you may be interested in these other books by Packt:

SAS for Finance
Harish Gulati

ISBN: 9781788624565

- Understand time series data and its relevance in the financial industry
- Build a time series forecasting model in SAS using advanced modeling theories
- Develop models in SAS and infer using regression and Markov chains
- Forecast inflation by building an econometric model in SAS for your financial planning
- Manage customer loyalty by creating a survival model in SAS using various groupings
- Understand similarity analysis and clustering in SAS using time series data

Mastering Qlik Sense

Martin Mahler, Juan Ignacio Vitantonio

ISBN: 9781783554027

- Understand the importance of self-service analytics and the IKEA-effect
- Explore all the available data modeling techniques and create efficient and optimized data models
- Master security rules and translate permission requirements into security rule logic
- Familiarize yourself with different types of **Master Key Item(MKI)** and know how and when to use MKI.
- Script and write sophisticated ETL code within Qlik Sense to facilitate all data modeling and data loading techniques
- Get an extensive overview of which APIs are available in Qlik Sense and how to take advantage of a technology with an API
- Develop basic mashup HTML pages and deploy successful mashup projects

Leave a review - let other readers know what you think

Please share your thoughts on this book with others by leaving a review on the site that you bought it from. If you purchased the book from Amazon, please leave us an honest review on this book's Amazon page. This is vital so that other potential readers can see and use your unbiased opinion to make purchasing decisions, we can understand what our customers think about our products, and our authors can see your feedback on the title that they have worked with Packt to create. It will only take a few minutes of your time, but is valuable to other potential customers, our authors, and Packt. Thank you!

Index

X
XML files